Dark Peak Aircraft Wreck Walks

by John N. Merrill

Maps, sketches and photographs by John N. Merrill

"I hike the paths and trails of the world for others to enjoy."

© *John N. Merrill 2004*

Walk & Write Ltd.

The Aircraft Wreck Walks Series.

2004

Walk & Write Ltd.,
Marathon House,
Longcliffe, Nr. Matlock,
Derbyshire, England. DE4 4HN

Tel/Fax 01629 - 540991
email - marathonhiker@aol.com

Typeset and designed by John N. Merrill & Walk & Write Ltd.
Printed and handmade by John N. Merrill.

©
©Text - - John N. Merrill. 2002.
   Photographs, Maps & sketches - John N. Merrill. 2002

ISBN 1-903627-04-4
First published - September 2001. Reprinted - December 2002

British Library Cataloguing-in-Publication Data. A catalogue record of this book is available from the British Library.

Typeset in Times New Roman - bold, italic, and plain 11pt, 14pt and 18pt.

Please note - The maps in this guide are purely illustrative. You are encouraged to use the appropriate 1:25,000 O.S. map.

John Merrill has walked all the routes in this book. Meticulous research has been undertaken to ensure that this publication is highly accurate at the time of going to press. The publishers, however, cannot be held responsible for alterations, errors, omissions, or for changes in details given. They would welcome information to help keep the book up to date.

Cover design - by John N. Merrill - Walk & Write Ltd 2002
Cover photograph - Plane engine below the Woolpacks, by John N. Merrill.

A little about John N. Merrill

Few people have walked the earth's crust more than John Merrill with more than 180,000 miles in the last 32 years - the average person walks 75,000 miles in a lifetime. Apart from walking too much causing bones in his feet to snap, like metal fatigue, he has never suffered from any back, hip or knee problems. Like other walkers he has suffered from many blisters, his record is 23 on both feet! He wears out at least three pairs of boots a year and his major walking has cost over £125,000. This includes 100 pairs of boots costing more than £11,800 and over £1,900 on socks - a pair of socks last three weeks and are not washed!

His marathon walks in Britain include - -

Hebridean Journey....... 1,003 miles. Northern Isles Journey......913 miles.
Irish Island Journey ....1,578 miles.   Parkland Journey.......2,043 miles.
Land's End to John o' Groats.....1,608 miles.
The East of England Heritage Route - 450miles.

and in 1978 he became the first person to walk the entire coastline of Britain - 6,824 miles in ten months.

In Europe he has walked across Austria - 712 miles - hiked the Tour of Mont Blanc, the Normandy coast, the Loire Valley (450 miles), a high level route across the Augverne(230 miles) and the River Seine (200 miles) in France, completed High Level Routes in the Dolomites and Italian Alps, and the GR20 route across Corsica in training! Climbed the Tatra Mountains ,the Transylvanian Alps in Romania, and in Germany walked in the Taunus, Rhine, the Black Forest (Clock Carriers Way) and King Ludwig Way (Bavaria). He has walked across Europe - 2,806 miles in 107 days - crossing seven countries, the Swiss and French Alps and the complete Pyrennean chain - the hardest and longest mountain walk in Europe, with more than 600,000 feet of ascent! In 1998 he walked 1,100 miles along the pilgrimage route from Le Puy (France) to Santiago (Spain) and onto Cape Finisterre; in 2002 walked 700 miles from Seville to Santiago de Compostela. In 2003 he walked 650 miles through the length of Portual via Fatima to Santiago de Compostela (Spian); 400 miles from Oslo to Trondheim, following St. Olav's Way, and all the trails on the Hong Kong Islands.

In America he used The Appalachian Trail - 2,200 miles - as a training walk, before walking from Mexico to Canada via the Pacific Crest Trail in record time - 118 days for 2,700 miles. Recently he walked most of the Continental Divide Trail and much of New Mexico; his second home. In 1999 he walked the Chesopeake & Ohio Canal National Historical Trail. In 2,000 he became the first thru hiker to walk 1,340 miles around Ohio, following the Buckeye Trail. In Canada he has walked the Rideau Trail - Kingston to Ottowa - 220 miles and The Bruce Trail - Tobermory to Niagara Falls - 460 miles.

In 1984 John set off from Virginia Beach on the Atlantic coast, and walked 4,226 miles without a rest day, across the width of America to Santa Cruz and San Francisco on the Pacific coast. This is one of the finest and most memorable walks, being in modern history, the longest, hardest crossing of the U.S.A. in the shortest time - under six months (178 days). The direct distance is 2,800 miles.

Between major walks John is out training in his own area - The Peak District National Park. He has walked all of our National Trails many times - The Cleveland Way thirteen times and The Pennine Way four times in a year! He has been trekking in the Himalayas five times. He created more than forty challenge walks which have been used to raise more than £700,000 for charity. From his own walks he has raised over £110,000. He is author of more than 250 walking guides which he prints and publishes himself, His book sales are in excess of 3 1/2 million, He has created many long distance walks including The Limey Way, The Peakland Way, Dark Peak Challenge walk, Rivers' Way, The Belvoir Witches Challenge Walk, The Forest of Bowland Challenge. the Dore to New Mills Challenge Walk , the Lincolnshire Wolds "𝕭𝖑𝖆𝖈𝖐 𝕯𝖊𝖆𝖙𝖍" Challenge Walk and the Happy Hiker (White Peak) Challenge Walk. His new Pilgrim Walk Series includes the 36 mile, "Walsingham Way" - King's Lynn to Walsingham. His monthly walks appear in Derbyshire's "Reflections" magazine. In January 2003, he was honoured for his walking and writing, recieving a Honorary degree, Master of the University, from Derby University. He lectures extensively about his walking.

CONTENTS

INTRODUCTION

It never ceases to amaze me the number of planes - 30 different types - that crashed on the moorlands of Kinder, Bleaklow and Saddleworth moors, mostly during World War 11. What amazes me even more that despite walking across these moorlands hundreds of times, I never knew that nearby and in one case beside a path, were the wreckage of a plane. Some are just a small collection of items, while others have an incredible amount of wings, engines, wheels and fuselage spread over a large area, with a monument to the brave air crew.

The walks in this book take you to every crash site in the Dark Peak area. Some you will find easily while others need more care to locate - could be in the next clough! The walks have a two fold objective; firstly to walk, often on compass bearings across the moors, using your navigational skills. Secondly, to see at first hand where, usually a war plane, crashed and see what remains. The site is the burial ground of the aircrew and requires our respect. The wreckage is MOD property and should not be removed and should be left for others to find.

Walking and researching a book like this is a never ending joy and adds upto another chapter in the "Peak District" story. Unlike the White Peak sites - see my "*White Peak Aircraft Wreck Walks*" book - the plane remains were easily removed. Here on the harsh moorland, with no helicopters at the time, the wrecks remain to be seen. To complete the story I have included two sites near Marsden and the Flying Fortress Monument in Endcliffe Park, Sheffield.

I have endeavoured to work out logical walks encompassing a group of crash sites - some long; some hard. Details of which planes to be seen on each walk is given and at the rear of the book are individual specifications for the planes. I have refrained from giving full details of the why they crashed as Ron Collier's books - *Dark Peak Aircraft Wrecks - Vol One and Two* - give very full details and are a must to read.

Put on your boots and set off in clear weather and traverse by compass to locate the wrecks. The time allowed for each walk is very fluid for you can easily spend an hour either looking for or at each wreck site. Enjoy the walks and see for yourself where recent history was made, while crossing the high moors of the Peak District.

Happy walking!
John N. Merrill

5

ABOUT THE WALKS

Whilst every care is taken detailing and describing the walk in this book, it should be borne in mind that the countryside changes by the seasons and the work of man. I have described the walk to the best of my ability, detailing what I have found on the walk in the way of stiles and signs. Obviously with the passage of time stiles become broken or replaced by a ladder stile or even a small gate. Signs too have a habit of being broken or pushed over. All the route follow rights of way and only on rare occasions will you have to overcome obstacles in its path, such as a barbed wire fence or electric fence. On rare occasions rights of way are rerouted and these ammendments are included in the next edition.

The seasons bring occasional problems whilst out walking which should also be borne in mind. In the height of summer paths become overgrown and you will have to fight your way through in a few places. In low lying areas the fields are often full of crops, and although the pathline goes straight across it may be more practical to walk round the field edge to get to the next stile or gate. In summer the ground is generally dry but in autumn and winter, especially because of our climate, the surface can be decidedly wet and slippery; sometimes even gluttonous mud!

These comments are part of countryside walking which help to make your walk more interesting or briefly frustrating. Standing in a farmyard up to your ankles in mud might not be funny at the time but upon reflection was one of the highlights of the walk!

The mileage for each section is based on three calculations -

1. pedometer reading.
2. the route map measured on the map.
3. the time I took for the walk.

I believe the figure stated for each section to be very accurate but we all walk differently and not always in a straight line! The time allowed for each section is on the generous side and does not include pub stops etc. The figure is based on the fact that on average a person walks 2 1/2 miles an hours but less in hilly terrain.

FINDING A CRASH SITE -

I believe the grid references and instructions should bring you to each specific site. Several sites have a marker cairn closeby, others have monuments, but nearly all have a cairn of remains. Whilst others have nothing but a scattering of fragments. Each site is different! Most are situated in peat groughs which require a careful search when the site's location is reached. A wander around the area will no doubt bring you to other pieces of wreckage. Two sites - the Gloster Meteors, on Sliddens Moss and the Sabre-F86's near Ashop Head, lie in "grass meadows" and can be seen from a long distance away. Sites like the Douglas Dakota which crashed in the rock face, has left its mark on the rocks but the wreckage/remains lie nearly 1/4 mile below. Sadly one wreck, the Liberator near Irontongue Hill, on Private Land, has been buried illegally. I hope no more suffer this fate.

Wellington - W8719 - crash site - Far Upper Tor., Kinder.
The middle rocks have a small plaque and below, left of centre,
the site and Remberance Day crosses.

KINDER AREA - CRASH LOCATIONS

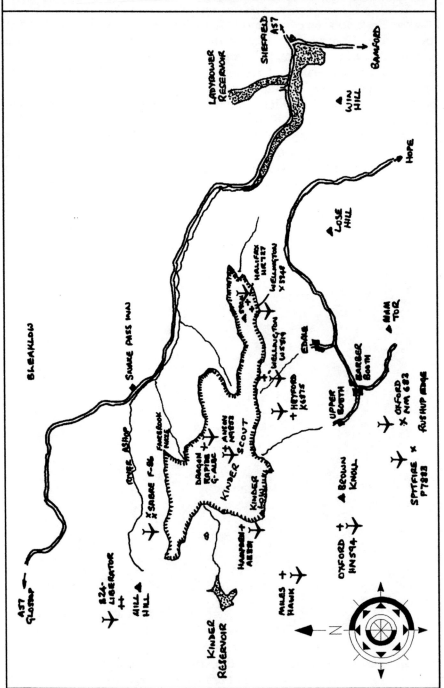

KINDER AIRCRAFT CRASH LOCATIONS -

PLANE	CRASH DATE	LOCATION	GRID REF.
Avro Anson - NL185	23/11/1945	The Cloughs	SK088866
North American Harvard.FT415	14/01/1952	The Woolpacks	SK088867 SK088869
Heyford - K6875	22/07/1937	Broadlee Bank Tor	SK111861
Wellington - X3348	26/01/1943	Blackden Edge - Trig 590m.	SK130877
Halifax - HR727	05/10/1943	Blackden Edge - Trig 590m.	SK132878
Dragon Rapide - G-ALBC	30/12/1963	Wove Hill - 623m.	SK102883
Avro Anson - N9853	11/12/1944	Edale Moor	SK102873
Airspeed Oxford -HN594	28/12/1945	Brown Knoll	SK083852
Thunderbolt - P47C	25/04/1943	Horsehill Tor	SK094845
Liberator B24	18/12/1943	Mill Hill	SK057907 SK058908
Sabre - F86 XD707&XD730	22/07/1954	Near Ashop Head	SK073904 SK077904
Hampden - AE381	21/01/1942	Cluther Rocks	SK078875
Wellington - W5719	31/07/1941	Far Upper Tor	SK875111
Spitfire - P7883	10/12/1943	Rushup Edge	SK108834
Oxford - NM683	04/03/1945	Rushup Edge	SK116837
Miles Hawk -Q-AJSF	29/07/1957	Oakenclough	SK074863

KINDER LOW & RUSHUP EDGE -10 MILES

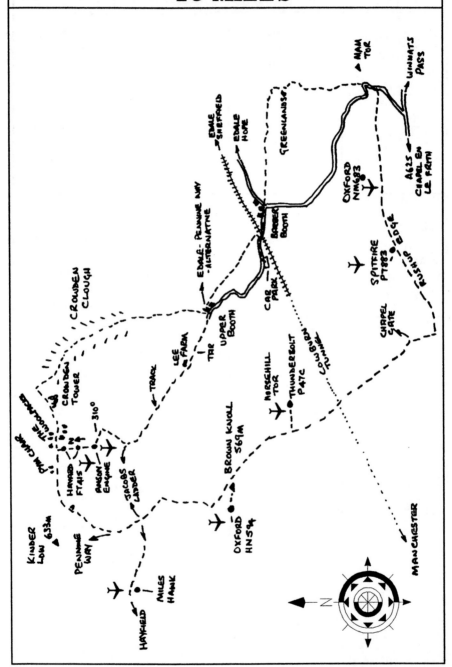

KINDER LOW , BROWN KNOLL(569m.) and RUSHUP EDGE
-600m of ascent
- 10 miles/17 km
- allow 6 hours

Basic Route - Barber Booth - Upper Booth - Crowden Clough - Crowden Tower - The Wool Packs - Pym Chair - Noe Stool - Swine's Back - Brown Knoll - Horsehill Tor - Rushup Edge - Mam Nick - Greenlands - Barber Booth.

 - 1:25,000 Outdoor Leisure Map No. 1 - The Dark Peak - West Sheet.

 Barber Booth. Grid Ref. SK109848.

 - None. Nearest at Edale -Rambler Inn. Ye Olde Nag's Head.

 - Upper Booth, and Edale.

ABOUT THE WALK - First a steep climb onto the Kinder Plateau near Crowden Tower - about an hours walk! Before reaching The Wool Packs and the first two crash sites. The route can be done from below to these sites, making there location easier to find. Next you head for the Hayfield bridlepath with the option of visiting the crash site of the Miles Hawk before aiming for the top of Brown Knoll - 569m. and the Oxford crash site nearby. You then head southwards to divert to the Thunderbolt site before continuing to Rushup Edge to pass the location of the two final sites. The views are magnificent; especially south and westwards.

WALKING INSTRUCTIONS - From the car park walk down the road - eastwards - to the railway viaduct and turn left over the footbridge over the River Noe. A few yards beyond turn left on a track to a stile. The pathline is now a defined path and well stiled to the hamlet of Upper Booth, 1/2 mile away, reached via a gate. Turn left past the buildings to the road and turn right. A few yards later turn right over a stile by a footpath sign, into Open Country. The path keeps to the lefthand side of Crowden Brook to a footbridge. Then on the righthand side to a stile and the ascent begins. The path keeps near to the brook and often fords it. High up the path divides - one keeps to the brook bed and involves scrambling in places. The other ascends steeply to the right of Crowden Tower. Whichever route you take turn left at the top for Crowden Tower, walking along the southern edge of Kinder Scout. Beyond the tower you enter the fascinating gritstone boulder area of the Wool Packs.

To the south of them towards The Cloughs are the remains of an **Avro Anson No. NL185**; H.Q. Flight R.A.F. Bomber Command; grid ref. 0905866; crashed 23/11/45 and a **North American Havard No. FT415**; Fleet Air Arm F.T.S.; grid ref. 089868 & 089867; crashed 14/1/52. Towards the end of the Wool Packs, turn due south to a shallow gully to the right of the gritstone edge. As you descend towards The Cloughs, you first come to the Havard site with large boulder closeby, carved - RAF 1952. Continue down the gully to more wreckage and finally onto the solitary Cheetah engine of the Anson. Retrace your steps back to up the gully to the Wool Packs and main path. Turn left and continue on the path to Pym Chair and onto the solitary stone - Noe Stool.

The lower route - *From Upper Booth keep on the Pennine Alternative path , first along the road to Lee Farm, with National Trust Information Centre. Continue on now on a track, using stiles, to reach the packhorse bridge before Jacob's Ladder, 1/2 mile away. Don't cross the bridge but turn right beside the brook for a short distance before turning right and ascend steeply, the grass slope with a fence on your right. In less than 1/4 mile where the terrain levels off, turn left on bearing 310° to reach the above gully area and the Cheetah Engine. Turn right and ascend the gully to the Harvard and onto the main Kinder perimeter path.*

Here the path descends past Edale Rocks and then beneath Swine's Back down to the bridleway from Jacob's Ladder. *(If you follow the track to your right for less than 1/2 mile past Edale Cross, you come to the crash site of the Miles Hawk - Q-AJSF, crashed 29/07/1957 at the start of Oakenclough. There are no remains.)* Cross over to the stile and follow the stone slabbed path leading towards the summit of Brown Knoll - 569m. The path turns right then left for the summit. Some 300 feet due west of the summit, in a shallow clough, is the wreckage of an **Airspeed Oxford plane No. HN594/21PAFU**; grid ref. 082852; crashed 28/12/45. One of the engines was removed and is on display in the Glossop Heritage Museum. Retrace your steps back to the trig point.

From the summit head south-easterly on a defined path - your goal is towards Rushup Edge 1 1/2 miles away. In more than 1/2 mile the path divides; keep to the lefthand one around the edge of the plateau. In more than 1/4 mile to your left - due east - on the southern slopes of Horsehill Tor can be seen a cairn - erected by the National Trust in memory of John Charles Gilligan by his family - *"I will lift mine eyes upto the hills."* 200 feet beyond and above the clough, down to Dalehead, can be seen a small mound of wreckage of a **Republic Thunderbird No. P47C.** 416227; 63 Fighter Sqdn USAAF; grid ref. 0935844; crashed 25.4.43.

Return to the main path and follow it south-easterly and in more than 1/2 mile reach the track - Chapel Gate. Turn right to reach the Rushup Edge path close to footpath sign No. 124 - Castleton-Hayfield. Turn left on the defined path slowly ascending and in 1/2 mile at the start of the "summit", on your left is the site where the **Spitfire - P7883** - crashed 10/12/1943. GR SK108834; there are no remains. Continue on the path passing "Lord's Seat" and begin gradually descending along the edge. In 1/4 mile on your left the slope falls steeply and here on these slopes an **Oxford - NM683** crashed here 04/03/1945. GR SK116837. I have searched in vain and found no wreckage.

Continue on the path to the road at Mam Nick. Turn left and in a few yards right to a stile. Over this keep left with a wall on your left as you descend to a stile. The path is well defined as you descend and swings right then left to a stile opposite Greenlands. Here gain the lane and turn right descending it following round to your left to a wooded hollow where it turns right. Here on your left are steps to a stile on your left. Ascend these and continue due west across the well stiled fields to the road junction near Barber Booth, 1/2 mile away. Keep straight ahead on the Upper Booth road to regain the car park and start.

Aircraft Wrecks seen on this walk -

North American Havard - FT415 - Undercarriage strut & wreckage. (The Wool Packs).
Avro Anson - NL185 - Cheetah Engine. (The Cloughs).
Miles Hawk. - site only. (Oakenclough).
Oxford - HN594.Considerable wreckage in clough.(Brown Knoll). One engine in Glossop Heritage Museum.
Thunderbolt - P47C. Small mound of wreckage.(Horsehill Tor).
Spitfire - P7883. - site only. (Rushup Edge)
Oxford - NM683. - Some wreckage can be found at GR 109837; very steep location, to the N.W. and below Lord's Seat.
Hampden - X3154 - crashed on south side at GR 104830, on 21st. December 1940. (Rushup Edge) - Site only.

Cheetah Engine - Avro Anson - NL185 - The Cloughs.

Strut Undercarraige - N.A. Harvard - FT415 - The Wool Packs.

14

Airspeed Oxford - HN 594 - remains, near Brown Knoll.

Thunderbolt - P47C - remains, Near Horsehill Tor.

BLACKDEN EDGE & GRINDSBROOK KNOLL - 6 MILES

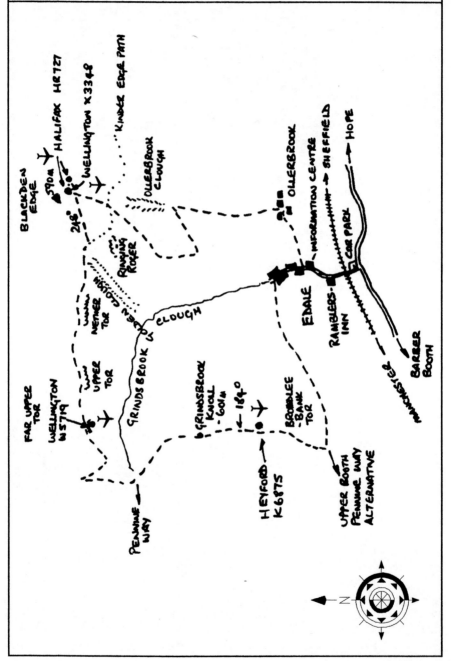

BLACKDEN EDGE & GRINDSBROOK KNOLL
- 6 MILES
- allow 4 hours

Route - Edale - Information Centre - Ollerbrook Booth - Ollerbrook Clough - Trig Point 590m. - Nether Tor - Upper Tor - Far Upper Tor - Grindslow Knoll 601m. - Broadlee-Bank Tor - Pennine Way - Edale.

 -1:25,000 Outdoor Leisure Map No.1 - The Dark Peak - West Sheet.

 Edale.

 - The Rambler Inn, Ye Olde Nag's Head, Edale.

- Several in Edale.

ABOUT THE WALK - Although short you have a steady ascent onto the Kinder Plateau to see the first Wellington site close to another site of a Halifax; incredibly both planes crashed in almost the same place, nine months apart. A mile later along Kinder's edge you come to the second Wellington site at Far Upper Tor, with a plaque. Nearly 2 miles later after Grindslow Knoll you reach the last site of the day, a Heyford. From here you descend to the Pennine Way and return to Edale. Throughout the walk you have spectacular views of the Edale valley.

WALKING INSTRUCTIONS - From the car park gain the Edale village road and turn right along it. Pass the Rambler Inn on your left. Less than 1/4 mile later pass Fieldhead Information Centre and campsite on your right. Just after opposite the White House dated 1678, turn right as footpath signed with the cemetery just over the wall. Descend the path and cross Grinds Brook to a stile. Keep ahead on a track with the wall on your left then right as approach the hamlet of Ollerbrook Booth.

Go through a gate and turn left, as path signed, with Ollerbrook Barn on your right. The path, a grass track leads to Open Country. Keep the wall on your right as you gently ascend to stiles and a cluster of pine trees on your right. Here you gain a stile and enter Open Country. Continue ahead now at the start of Ollerbrook Clough. In a short distance follow the track round to your left as it ascends the slope of The Knab. On the crest it turns right and continues to ascend and in less than 1/4 mile keep right on a defined path that ascends beneath Ringing Roger to gain the edge of Kinder at the head of Ollerbrook Clough.

Keep straight ahead on bearing 38° to reach the trig point 590m. about 1/4 mile away. The first two sites, within 200 yards of each other, are just to your right. Bearing 126° brings you to **Wellington - X3348** - GR SK130877 - site with one cross, marking a handful of remains. Bearing 148° brings you to the **Halifax - HR727** - GR SK132878 - site with two cross, wreckage and armour plating. Return back to the trig point. Now on bearing 248° cross the moorland to regain the Kinder edge path near the head of Golden Clough. Keep on the edge path for the next mile passing the gritstone outcrops of Nether Tor and Upper Tor on your left. Little over 1/4 mile later gain Far Upper Tor with a clough beyond. Turn left and descend to the base of the rocks to find the remains of the **Wellington - W5719** - GR SK875111 - that crashed here. The rocks behind have a plaque - *"In memory of Wellington W5719 150 squadron RAF returning to base at Snaith from a raid in Cologne 31st. July 1941."*

Ascend back to the edge path and turn left along it following round the head of Grindsbrook Clough. Cross the Pennine Way path and soon afterwards bear right on a defined path (perimeter path). In 200 yards turn left to follow a smaller path that passes beneath the northern slopes of Grindslow Knoll. Follow it round to its southern end and continue ahead, now on bearing 184°. In more than 1/4 mile reach a stone wall on the edge of Broadlee-Bank Tor. A few yards to your left is a small cairn and remains of **Heyford - K6875** - GR SK111861. Return to the path and descend it down the slope of Broadlee-Bank Tor; on your left is a wall. At the bottom gain a stile and soon reach the alternative Pennine Way path from Edale. Turn left along following it back to Edale 3/4 mile away. Entering the village via a walled path to the "square" close to the Ye Olde Nag's Head opposite. Turn right and follow the road through the village past the church, Information Centre and Rambler Inn back to the car park.

Aircraft Wrecks seen on this walk -

Wellington - X3348 - crashed 26/01/1943 - small mound of remains.
Halifax - HR727 - crashed 5/10/1943 - wreckage and armour plating in shallow clough.
Wellington - W5719 - crashed 31/07/1941 - scrattered frgaments and plaque.
Heyford - K6875 - crashed 22/07/1937 - small mound of remains.

Wellington - X3348 - remains.

19

Halifax - HR727 - Radiator.

Halifax - HR727 - Main wreckage and armour plating at top.

Wellington - W5719 - a few remains.

Heyford - K6875 - cairn and remains.

FAIRBROOK, MILL HILL & SNAKE PATH - 12 MILES

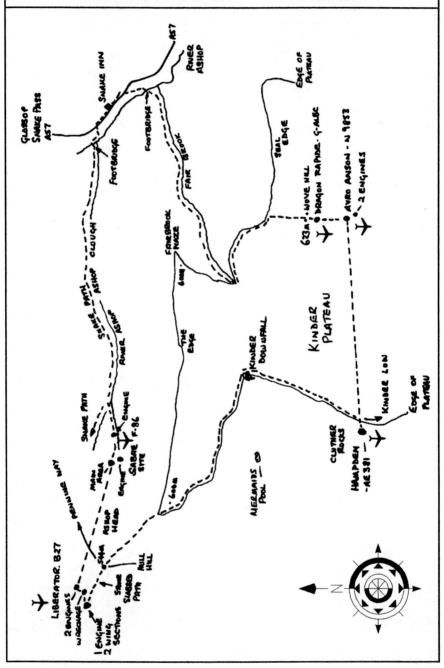

FAIRBROOK, MILL HILL & SNAKE PATH
- 12 MILES
- allow 8 hours.

Route - A57 (Snake Inn) - Fairbrook - Kinder Plateau - Seal Edge - Wove Hill - Edale Moor - Cluther Rocks - Pennine Way - Kinder Downfall - Mill Hill - Snake Path - Ashop Clough - River Ashop - A57 (Snake Inn).

 - 1:25,000 Outdoor Leisure Map No.1 - The Dark Peak - West Sheet.

 - Road side parking beside A57, south of Snake Inn.

 - The Snake Inn.

ABOUT THE WALK - A hard walk bringing you to the finest wreck sites and country on Kinder Scout. First you ascend onto the Kinder plateau via the beautiful Fair Brook. From here you walk along the northern rim before crossing the moorland on compass bearings to Wove Hill to find the cylinder block from a Dragon Rapide - G-ALBC. A little further south is the wreckage and two engines of the Avro Anson - N9853. Here you head westwards across Kinder Scout on a fixed bearing for 1 1/2 miles over easy terrain to Kinder's western edge and the Hampden - AE381 site - above and east of Cluther Rocks. Now on the Pennine Way you follow it to Kinder Downfall and onto Mill Hill. Westwards from here are the impressive remains of a B24 Liberator. One final bearing eastwards brings you to two Sabre F-86 wreckage and jet engines. You return down the Snake Path back to the A57 and Snake Inn.

WALKING INSTRUCTIONS - Walk down the A57 road from the Snake Inn, and 1/4 mile from it is a stile and footpath sign - "Open Country" - on your right. Descend the path through pine trees to a footbridge over the River Ashop, and enter *"Fairbrook - High Peak Estate"* - National Trust Property. Bear left before turning right on the path close to Fair Brook on your left. Begin the gradual ascent of Fair Brook along a good path beside and above the brook on your left. After 3/4 mile of gradual ascent it becomes steeper as you ascend on the right of the brook to the edge of the Kinder plateau and perimeter path. Turn left along it towards Seal Edge, but before you get there - after about 15 minutes of walking turn south on bearing 196° for Wove Hill, 623m. Not named on the map but a small rocky hillock, which takes about 15 minutes to reach. On the other side, at the bottom is the engine block from **Dragon Rapide - G-ALBC** - GR SK102883. Before you descend to find it look southwards over Edale Moor for there on the other side of the "hollow" is your next site.

First descend and find the cylinder block then go on compass bearing 182° for approximately 10 minutes. Cross a path and ascend slightly to peat groughs. Here in the groughs are two engines and wreckage of the **Avro Anson -N9853** - GR SK102873. Now turn westwards on bearing 266° for almost 1 1/2 miles, across Kinder Scout passing spot height 636m. to the perimeter path (Pennine Way) on its western edge. Here on the righthand side of the path are two small piles of remains of the **Hampden - AE381**. GR SK078875. Turn right along the Pennine Way following the distinct path along the edge of Kinder to Kinder Downfall. Continue round, north-westerly on the path for another mile, before descending steeply down to Ashop Head. Continue ahead, still on the Pennine Way, and now on a stone slabbed path to the summit of Mill Hill, 644m.

Here leave the Pennine Way, which swings right, and follow the slabbed path westwards on bearing 300°. In about five minutes of gentle descent you reach the start of the extensive remains of the **B24 Liberator** - GR SK057907 & SK058908. First on the right of the path is an engine and two large wing sections. Turn right on bearing 64° for two minutes to find more wreckage, including two engines and the undercarriage. Now head southeasterly on bearing 120° for almost a mile. First crossing the Pennine Way then descending across Ashop Head and across moorland beneath Kinder's northern edge. Here you find considerable wreckage from the two **Sabre's F-86 - XD707 & XD730** that crashed here - GR. SK073904 & SK077904. A search will find one engine further east in a grough, with another 1/4 mile away on bearing 86° in a bog. This bearing will also bring you to the Snake Path, less than 1/4 mile away. Turn right along the path and follow it descending down Ashop Clough to pine trees and footbridge over the brook from Bleaklow. Follow the path right then left and ascend to the A57 road. Turn right to the Snake Inn and roadside parking area

Aircraft Wrecks seen on this walk -

Dragon Rapide - G-ALBC - crashed 30/12/1963 - engine block and wreckage.

Avro Anson - N9853 - crashed 11/12/1944 - two engines and wreckage.

Hampden - AE381 - crashed 21/01/1942 - two small mounds of wreckage and plaque.

B24 Liberator - crashed 18/12/1943 - large amount of wreckage - engines, wings and undercarriage.

Sabre - F86 - XD707 & XD730 - crashed 22/07/1954 - considerable wreckage, wheels and jet engines.

Dragon Rapide - G-ALBC - Cylinder block.

25

Hampden - AE381 - wreckage mound.

Hampden - AE381 - Memorial Cross.

B24 Liberator - Wing section.

B24 Liberator - Engine

Sabre - F86 - Wing Sections.

Sabre - F86 - Wreckage pile and memorial plaque.

Sabre - F86 - Landing wheel.

Sabre - F86 - Engine remains.

29

BLEAKLOW AREA - CRASH SITES

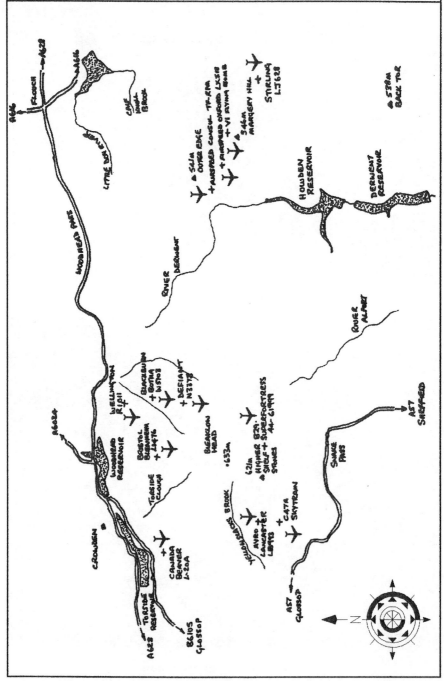

BLEAKLOW AIRCRAFT CRASH LOCATIONS -

PLANE	CRASH DATE	LOCATION	GRID REF.
V1 - Flying Bomb	24/12/1944	Cut Gate/ FeatherbedMoss	SK187965
Short Stirling -LJ 628	21/07/1944	Stainery Clough	SK202957 SK202958 SK203957
Airspeed Oxford-LX518	19/10/1943	Broadhead Clough Head	SK180968
Consul -TF-RPM	12/05/1951	Crowstones Edge (S. of)	SK174966
Wellington - R1011	30/01/1943	Birchen Bank Moss	SK105986
Boulton Paul Defiant-3378	29/08/1941	Nr. Bleaklow Stones	SK110972 SK108969
Bristol Blenheim.L1476	30/01/1943	Wildboar Clough	SK079976 SK080977
Canada Beaver -L20A	05/12/1956	Bramah Edge	SK055976
N.A. Sabre -F86	18/12/1954	Great Hill	SK092051 SK090050
Superfortress 44-61999	03/11/1948	Higher Shelf Stones	SK091948
Lancaster -LB993	18/05/1945	James Thorn	SK078947
Skytrain C47A	24/07/1945	Ashton Clough	SK081945 SK082941
Blackburn Botha - W5103	10/12/1941	Round Hill	SK109978
Wellington - DV810	9/12/1942	Broomhead Moor	SK232954
Avro Anson - N9912	31/03/1941	Whitwell Moor	SK249978

HIGHER SHELF STONES
- 5 MILES

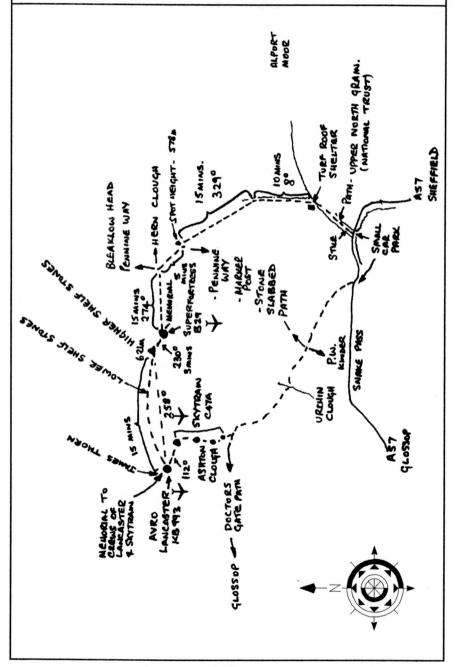

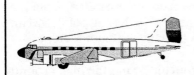

HIGHER SHELF STONES
- 5 MILES
- allow 3 to 4 hours.

Route - A57 - Upper North Grain - Pennine Way (Alport Low) - Hern Clough - Superfortress - Higher Shelf Stones - 621m - Lower Shelf Stones - James Thorn - Ashton Clough - Doctor's gate - Pennine Way - A57 - Upper North Grain.

- O.S. 1:25,000 Outdoor Leisure Map No 1 - The Dark Peak - West Sheet.

- Small parking area on the Snake Pass road - A57 - 1/2 mile from summit at Upper North Grain. Grid Ref. SK 0101929.

- None - nearest Snake Inn on the A57 road, 2 miles south.

ABOUT THE WALK - A short moorland walk onto Bleaklow crossing the Pennine Way. You follow compass bearing to the head of Hern Clough and onto Higher Shelf Stones - 621m. Before the summit you reach the Peak District's largest crash site - B24 Superfortress - AA-61999. From Higher Shelf Stones you continue on a compass bearing to James Thorn and the site of Lancaster - KB993. Here you descend steeply down Ashop Clough to see the scattered remains of a Skytrain C47A. At the bottom of the clough you pick up Doctor's Gate and follow it back to the A57 and car park. The monument at James Thorn is too both the Lancaster and Skytrain crews.

WALKING INSTRUCTIONS - From the A57 road at Upper North Grain, go through a stile and follow a path, with the stream on your left, into National Trust property - "Upper North Grain." In just over 1/4 mile reach a Y junction of drainage streams with a turf roof shelter on your left. Here bear left (northwards) on bearing 8° for approximately 10 minutes. Then turn left on bearing 329° and in about 15 minutes you should reach the Pennine Way, near spot height 578m. Follow the Pennine Way for 5 minutes to the head of Hern Clough on your right. Turn left (westwards) on bearing 274° and ascend the moorland for a 1/3 mile to the crash site where **Superfortress B-29** "Over Exposed" - GR SK090950 - crashed on 3rd. November 1948; all thirteen crew were killed. A plaque details the names. After exploring the site ascend to the trig point, 621m. on the summit of Higher Shelf Stones, on bearing 230°, and views.

Continue westwards on bearing 258° contouring round the high ground to Lower Shelf Stones and onto James Thorn (15 minutes), the end the high ground. Here is the plaque to the **Lancaster - KB993** - GR SK078947 and Skytrain and a lot of small molten fragments of the Lancaster, that burnt ferociously on impact. Turn left, southeasterly, on bearing 112°, and descend steeply to Ashton Clough, passing wreckage of the **C47A Skytrain** - GR SK081945 & SK082941. In the clough first come to half buried tail section. Continue descending the clough coming to more pieces of the plane - engines, wheel and at the bottom further wreckage. Cross the level section to gain Doctor's Gate path and turn left ascending. In 1/2 mile reach the junction with the Pennine Way. Keep straight ahead on Doctor's Gate path and in less than 1/2 mile reach the A57. Turn left and descend to Upper North Grain.

Doctor's Gate Path - the Roman Road that linked the Roman Forts of Navio near Brough in the Hope Valley with Melandra at Glossop.

Plane wrecks seen on this walk -

Boeing Superfortress B29 - Site Grid Ref. SK090950. Crashed 03/11/1948. There is a monument to the thirteen crew members who were killed. Scattered around the area can be seen wings, engines, fuselage and landing gear. The bomber is famous for being used to drop the atomic bombs on Japan on the 4th and 9th August 1945. This plane was used in the atomic group for photography purposes.
Lancaster KB993 - crashed 18/05/1945 - plaque and molten remains.
Skytrain C47A - crashed 24/07/1945 - fuselage, engines and wheels scattered in Ashton Clough.

AVRO LANCASTER AND SKYTRAIN CRASH REMAINS LOCATIONS - ASHTON CLOUGH.

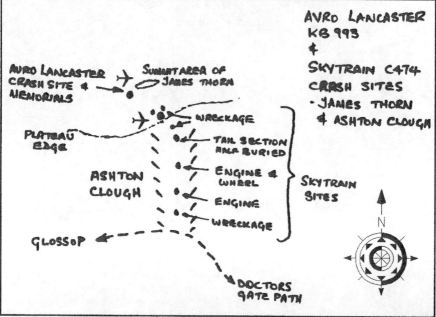

AVRO LANCASTER
KB 993
&
SKYTRAIN C474
CRASH SITES
- JAMES THORN
& ASHTON CLOUGH

AVRO LANCASTER
CRASH SITE & MEMORIALS

SUMMIT AREA OF JAMES THORN

WRECKAGE

PLATEAU EDGE

TAIL SECTION HALF BURIED

ASHTON CLOUGH

ENGINE & WHEEL

ENGINE

WRECKAGE

SKYTRAIN SITES

GLOSSOP

DOCTORS GATE PATH

N

Skytrain tail section in Ashton Clough.

Superfortress - Landing gear.

Superfortress - Engines and radiator.

36

Lancaster remains at James Thorn
- Skytrain and Lancaster plaque beyond.

Skytrain engine in Ashton clough.

BLEAKLOW HEAD - 633M -15 MILES

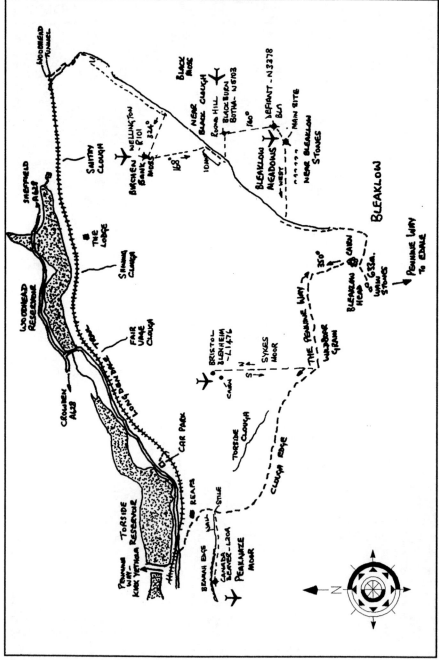

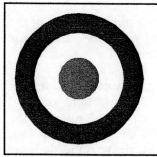

BLEAKLOW HEAD
- 633 M
- 600m of ascent
13 miles / 20 km
- allow 6 to 7 hours.

Route - Torside Reservoir Car Park - Longdendale Trail - Woodhead Tunnel - Near Black Clough - Birchen Bank Moss - Wellington - R1011 - crash site - Near Black Clough - Round Hill - Blackburn Botha - W5103 - crash site - Defiant - N3378 - crash site - Near Bleaklow Stones - Black Clough - Bleaklow Head Cairn - Wain Stones - Cairn - Pennine Way - Wildboar Grain - Bristol Blenheim - L1476 - crash site - Wildboar Grain - Clough Edge - Reaps - Longdendale Trail - Car Park.

- One mile extension from above Reaps to Bramah Edge and Canada Beaver - L 20 A crash site.

- I : 25,000 Outdoor Leisure Map No. 1 - The Dark Peak - West Sheet.

- Close to Longdendale Trail off the B6105 road. Grid Ref. SK069983. There are toilets here and an Information Centre (open weekends only).

Food - None - carry what you need. Seasonal refreshments in car park.

ABOUT THE WALK - A great day's walk in high moorland with beautiful views. I saw no one on the day I did it except for a lone Pennine Way walker! Choose a clear settled day for the walk to four different crash sites. Bleaklow Head is not a dramatic summit - just the highest point of the peat moorland and Peak District - but the walk up Black Clough is exceptional and the descent along the Pennine Way above Torside Reservoir is a rewarding "mountain" walk. You also walk a major section of the Longdendale Trail which forms part of the E8 Trans Pennine Walk from Liverpool and Hull AND onto Istanbul more than 2,500 miles away - I hope to walk it some day! You walk the trail first as a lull before the ascent. You will no doubt see many startled red grouse and in winter the *"white"* mountain hares. In August the heather is in full bloom and cloudberry grows substantially. Have a good walk and enjoy one of the finest areas of the Peak District. The last time I was here I sat on the Botha surrounded by snow, letting in the New Year!

WALKING INSTRUCTIONS - From the car park walk up to its top lefthand corner to the path to the Longdendale Trail. Gaining the trail turn left and basically keep on the trail for more than 3 miles to the entrance to Woodhead Tunnel. After a mile pass the site of Crowden Station; in use from July 1861 to February 1957. At the Woodhead tunnel turn right along the track towards the A628 road but before it turn right over a bridge over the River Etherow to a stile on your left. Over this keep the river on your left as you walk along a track. Follow the track round to your right with the river on your left and pass some delightful ponds. Keep ahead as the track becomes a path and follow it round to your right ascending the side of the clough to the top. Turn left along a good path along the top and after about 15 minutes leave the path and turn right on bearing 324° and in about 14 minutes should reach the **Wellington - R1011** - crash site - GR SK105986 - marked by a cairn and monument -

> *"In memory of Sergeant Raymond Rouse, Flying Officer Lane, and Pilot Officer Brown, who tragically lost their lives, when their aircraft a Vickers Armstrong Wellington No. R1011 crashed into the ground at this site on 30th January 1943."*

Turn left, heading southwards on bearing 168° back to Near Black Clough and descend to the brook beneath Round Hill. Turn right beside it and in ten minutes at a prominent clough on your left, turn left and ascend eastwards to the summit of Round Hill. 100 yards south-east of the flat summit will be found the large single remain - wing section - of the **Blackburn Botha - W5103** - G.R. SK109978. Continue southwards on bearing 160° ascending gently and in ten minutes come to metal parts in a grough from the **Defiant N3378** - GR SK110972. Continue ascending to your right for five minutes to Near Bleaklow Stones - GR SK108969 - where you will find the main crash site, cairn and scattered fragments.

> *" Pilot Officer James Craig and George Hempstead lost lives in a Boulton Paul Defiant No. 3378. Crashed into the ground at this site on 29th August 1941."*

Head due west and in less than 1/2 mile reach the main path in Black Clough; you are now high on Bleaklow. Keep beside the stream bed following it to a fence and stile. Continue following the widest channel as it curves right (westwards) towards the large cairn on Bleaklow Head.

This is almost the highest point but 200 yards to the south-west is a stake and the Wain Stones at the highest point. After your visit return to the large cairn and as written on a rock are now on the Pennine Way follow the path almost northwards on bearing 350°.

The path is well defined now and in 1/4 mile the path swings left - almost due west - and descends Wildboar Grain. Where the path crosses the stream to continue on the Pennine Way keeping high above Torside Clough along Clough Edge, turn right and head due north across Sykes Moor. In about 20 minutes you should see a prominent cairn, above a grough, marking the area of the **Bristol Blenheim - L1476** - site - GR. SK079977. The main site is a little further beyond with considerable wreckage, two engines and monument -

> "645 Sqdn RAF crashed 30/01/1943. Killed the two crew - Plt Officer S.J.D. Robinson. Act. Plt Off. J.E.Thomas."

Retrace your steps due south back to Wildboar Grain and the Pennine Way. Turn right along Clough Edge above Torside Clough. In 1 1/4 miles descend to the Open Country entry point and stile. Here you can turn left, heading due west over rough ground for 1/2 mile to the middle of Bramah Edge and the **Canada Beaver L-20A** site - GR. SK 065976. I have searched the base of the edge for any remains, but found nothing. Return to the entry point and stile and continue on the path towards the farm - Reaps - and then keep left on the farm drive to near the Glossop road. Before it turn right, as signed and right again onto the Longdendale Trail. Keep on the trail for 3/4 mile to the path to the car park. Turn left and retrace your steps back to it.

Aircraft wreck sites seen on this walk -

Wellington - R101 - Birchen Bank Moss - crashed 30/01/1943 - Cairn, monument and fragments.
Blackburn Botha - W5103 - Round Hill - crashed 10/12/1941 - large single piece of wing section.
Boulton Paul Defiant - N3378 - crashed into ground, near Bleaklow Bleaklow Stones - 29/08/1941 - scattered remains and monument.
Bristol Blenheim - L1476 - crashed 30/01/1943 - above Wildboar Clough - Monument, cairn, lot of wreckage and two engines.
Canada Beaver - L-20A - crashed 05/12/1956 - Crash location; no remains.

41

In Memory Of Sergeant Raymond Rouse, Flying Officer Lane, And Pilot Officer Brown, Who Tragically Lost Their Lives, When Their Aircraft A Vickers Armstrong Wellington No R1011 Crashed Into The Ground At This Site On 30th January 1943.

Wellington - R1011 - cairn, remains and monument.

Blackburn Botha - W5103 - wing section; in the snow.

Boulton Paul Defiant - 3378 - wreckage in clough before main site.

Boulton Paul Defiant - 3378 - main site and memorial.

Bristol Blenheim - L1476 - memorial and wreckage.

Bristol Blenheim - L1476 - Memorial, wreckage and engine.

Bramah Edge - crash site of Canada Beaver - L20A.

MARGERY HILL - 546m
and Outer Edge - 541m - 12 MILES

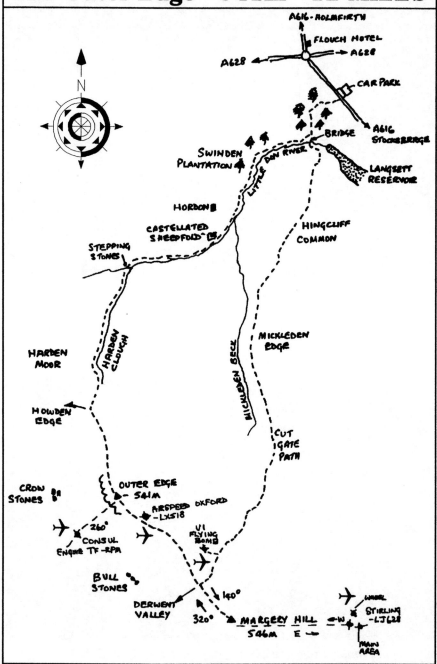

MARGERY HILL - 546m & OUTER EDGE - 541m
- 400m of ascent
- 12 miles / 20 km
- allow 6 hours

Route - Flouch Car Park (A616) - Crookland Wood - Hingcliff Common - Mickleden Edge - Cut Gate Path - V1 Flying Bomb site - Cut Gate - Margery Hill 546m - Short Stirling J628 site - Margery Hill - Cut Gate - Airspeed Oxford - LX518 site - Outer Edge - 541m - Consul - TF-RPM site - Outer Edge - Harden Clough - Little Don River - Crookland Wood - A616.

- 1:25,000 Outdoor Leisure Map - The Dark Peak - East Sheet.

- 1/4 mile south of Flouch Hotel - Yorkshire Water Langsett (Flouch) Car Park just off the A616 road. Grid Ref. SK202013.

- None. Nearest in Flouch or Langsett. Carry what you need.

ABOUT THE WALK - A wonderful moorland walk! First you walk through pine trees to the Little Don River before starting the gradual ascent along the Cut Gate Path past Mickleden Edge and V1 site, on the right, to the cairn on Howden Edge. Here you turn left to ascend Margery Hill - 546m. 3/4 mile due east of here are the extensive remains of the Short Stirling site. You return to Margery Hill and back to the cairn on Howden Edge and cross moorland towards the trig point on the summit of Outer Edge - 541m. On the way on your right are the small remains of an Airspeed Oxford. You head west to the Consul site before gaining the trig point on Outer Edge, 541m and descend the other side having once more admired the views - especially to Mam Tor. 1/2 mile of walking you turn northwards and descend a delightful path down Harden Clough to the Little Don River. You follow this back to the pine trees - a particularly attractive section - and retrace your steps back to the A616 and car park. A truly exceptional day out in quiet moorland - I only saw two people - in the distance - all day!

Please note - The Short Stirling crash site is on Private land and full respect should be shown.

WALKING INSTRUCTIONS - Exit the car park via the top righthand corner - as signed near an Information board. Cross the A616 road to a track and bridlepath sign. Keep straight ahead into the pine trees. Follow the track for less than 1/4 mile to the next path sign. Turn left here still on a track and pass another bridlepath to your left - the path on your right is your return path. Keep ahead and in a few yards bear right and descend the track to the bridge over the Little Porter River with Langsett Reservoir to your left. Follow the track round to your left then right as you ascend to Open Country. Keep straight ahead and in 1/4 mile pass a track to your left at spot height 322m. Keep ahead across Hingcliff Common as the track now becomes a path. In 3/4 mile pass another Open Country sign as you continue on the path onto Mickleden Edge with Mickleden Beck below on your right. In a further 1/4 mile pass the Peak District Footpath preservation Societies Footpath plaque No. 50 dated 1925. This sign has stood here over seventy years - doesn't it make sense to make the present day signs in the same way, rather than wood which last a few years?

Keep ahead gently ascending - Cut Gate Path - for more than two miles to the cairn on the edge of Howden Edge - Cut Gate. Before the cairn and after about 1 3/4 miles (1/4 mile from Howden Edge) turn due west for 200 yards to the **V1 Flying bomb** site - GR. SK187965. There is nothing to see except for peat filled crater. Return east back to the path and continue to the cairn on Howden Edge. Here the views unfold southwards over Kinder and the Hope Valley - Mam Tor looks spectacular from here! Turn left - 140° - and in little over 1/4 mile reach the triangulation pillar on the summit of Margery Hill - 546 m. Margery Stones are just ahead.

From the stones head due east, descending gently down the moorland towards Stainery Clough. In about 20 minutes you should start seeing wreckage from the **Short Stirling - LJ628** - GR. SK203956/7 and SK203957. There is considerable amount with a landing wheel further down. Return due west retracing your steps back to Margery Stones and hill. Retrace your steps back to the cairn on Howden Edge - 320°. Continue on this bearing to cross moorland - the path is defined and sometimes staked - and cross a ford. 1/4 mile later (5 minutes) on your right - 40 yards from the path in a small clough are the few remains of the **Airspeed Oxford - LX518** - GR. SK180968. From here head west on bearing 260° and in ten minutes you should reach the engine and remains from the **Consul - TF-RPM** - GR. SK174966. Head north-easterly on bearing 54° to the triangulation pillar on the summit of Outer Edge - 541 m., 10 minutes away. As you walked to your left are the Bull Stones and Crow

Stones Edge.

Gain the main path and continue on it heading northwards as you descend gently. In more than 1/4 mile pass a boundary stone with the letter R on. 300 yards later pass another and in a few yards turn right and walk along the lefthand side of Harden Clough. The path is not obvious at first but in 100 yards as you descend along the lefthand side of the clough it becomes well defined; you are in Open Country. In more than a mile reach the bottom with stone walled fields ahead and Hordron Clough to your left. Cross the Little Don River via the stepping stones and turn right. Keep the river on your right as you follow a small path. In 1/4 mile pass on your left an impressive castellated sheepfold. In another mile turn left then right to continue on the lefthand side of the river. 1/4 mile later reach a bridlepath sign and Open Country sign. Go through the stile and turn right following a path beside a wall with the river below on your right. Descend to the river and walk through pine trees to a stile. Continue on the path which soon brings you to your start out path/ track. Turn left along it and then right to regain the A616 road. Cross over to the car park.

Aircraft Wrecks seen on this walk -

V1 Flying bomb - Featherbed Moss - crashed 24/12/1944. Peat filled in crater only.

Short Stirling - LJ628 - Stainery Clough - crashed 21/07/ 1944. Considerable wreckage - wings, fuselage and tyred wheels.

Airspeed Oxford - LX518 - Broadhead Clough Head - crashed 19/10/1943. Scattered remains.

Consul - TF-RPM - Crowstones Edge - crashed 12/05/1951. Scattered remains and engine.

V1 Flying Bomb crash site - Featherbed Moss.

Short Stirling - LJ 628 - Main wreckage.

Short Stirling - LJ 628 - Main wreckage.

Short Stirling - LJ 628 - tyred landing wheel.

Airspeed Oxford - LX 518 - scattered remains.

Airspeed Consul - TF-RPM - main remains, memorial and engine.

BROOMHEAD MOOR - 3 MILES & WHITWELL MOORS - 5 MILES

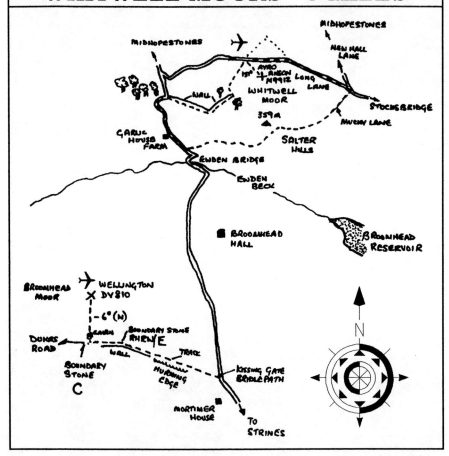

BROOMHEAD MOOR - 3 MILES - Start from the summit of Hurkling Edge, above Mortimer House - GR. SK245945. Turn left at bridlepath sign and kissing gate. Follow the defined track - Dukes Road - for 3/4 mile to a large cairn. In little over 1/2 mile you have an intermittent wall on your left and pass boundary stone - RHRW - with a large E on the otherside, on your right. Soon after reach a large cairn on your right with another boundary stone ahead with the letter C. Turn right, northwards - 6° and in about 10 minutes across peat moorland, you should reach the **Wellington - DV810** - crash site. Return the same way.

BROOMHEAD MOOR - 3 MILES & WHITWELL MOOR - 5 MILES - allow 1 and 2 hours.

ABOUT THE WALKS - Near the north-eastern corner of the Peak District, on the slopes of Bleaklow are the location where two planes came down. On **Broomhead Moor at GR SK232954 a Wellington - DV810 -** crashed 9/12/1942. Little over 2 miles north-east on **Whitwell Moor - Avro Anson - N9912 -** crashed 31/03/1941. Both sites are on Private Land. For the keen wreck historian I include them as two separate short walks to see their crash sites; both have a small amount of wreckage. The walks are covered by 1:25,000 Outdoor Leisure Map No.1 - The Dark Peak - East Sheet. Roadside parking only.

WHITWELL MOOR - 5 MILES - Starting near Ewden Bridge - GR SK243968 - ascend the road a short distance to a gate and bridlepath sign on your right. Follow the path across the field to a gate and wall. Keep beside the wall for a short distance before walking through woodland to Salt Spring Beck and back into fields. Keep a hedge on your right and gently traverse across another stream and ascend to a stile, with Nether House Farm to your right. Continue to another stile and path sign as you ascend a track to the top of Salter Hills. Follow it round to your right and path crossroads. Take the half-right, ascending path over the "hill" to a wall and Mucky Lane. Soon reach a stile and continue ahead on a walled path to the road junction at The Poplars. Turn left along Long Lane - *"To Strines"*. In more than 1/4 mile the road turns left and on the right a path crosses the field to the track called Peg Folly. Turn left along the path back to Long Lane and ladder stile opposite. You ascend this path on the right of the trees, but the **Avro Anson - N9912 -** crash site lies south-east on bearing 151° - about 8 minutes walk over rough ground - GR. SK249978. Return same way back to path and turn left and ascend to a wall and woodland and a stile. Go through and soon bear left then right and descend to a stone stile. Continue ahead out of the wood and by a wall on your right to a stile. Turn right and keep the wall on your right to three stiles and path sign - Bolsterstone - and Ewden Bridge road. Turn left and descend the road back to the bridge.

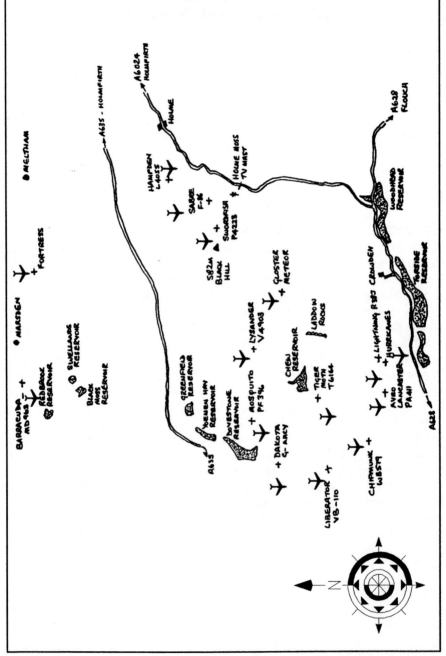

CHEW & MARSDEN AIRCRAFT CRASH LOCATIONS -

PLANE	CRASH DATE	LOCATION	GRID REF.
Fairy Swordfish - P4223	25/01/1940	Heyden Head	SK083048
Glosters Meteor- WA971	12/04/1951	Sliddens Moss	SK068028
Sabre - F86E	14/12/1954	Black Hill	SK091051
Hampden -L4055	23/05/1940	Round Hill west of Holme	SK098058
Lightning - P38J	10/05/1944	Tintwistle Knarr	SK040993
Hurricanes -PZ851, PZ765 PZ853	22/11/1945	Didsbury Intake	SK036988
Avro Lancaster- PA411	20/12/1948	Rhodes Hill	SK034994
Chipmunk -WB579	03/07/1951	Arnfield Moor	SK027997
Liberator - VB-110	19/12/1943	Irontongue Hill	SK017009
Tiger Moth - T6161	12/04/1945	Chew Brook	SK035016
Dakota G-AHCY	19/08/1949	Wimberry Stones	SK014025
Mosquito - PF395	22/10/1944	Dean Rocks	SK024033
Lysander -V9403	19/08/1941	Slate Pit Moss	SK041033
Barracuda -MD963	29/07/1945	Redbrook Clough	SK024104
Fortress B-17G-65	06/04/1945	Meltham Moor	SK071097

BLACK HILL - 582m - 13 MILES

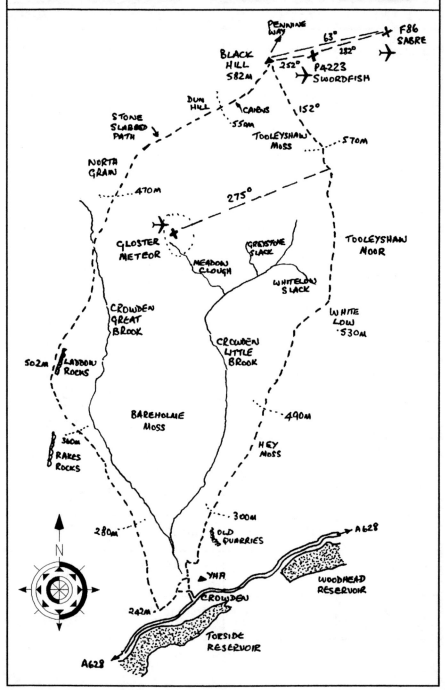

PENNINE WAY

F86 SABRE

63°

282°

252°

P4223 SWORDFISH

BLACK HILL 582M

152°

DUN HILL

CAIRNS

550M

STONE SLABBED PATH

TOOLEYSHAW MOSS

570M

NORTH GRAIN

470M

275°

GLOSTER METEOR

MEADOW CLOUGH

GREYSTONE SLACK

TOOLEYSHAW MOOR

WHITELOW SLACK

CROWDEN GREAT BROOK

WHITE LOW ·530M

502M LADDOW ROCKS

CROWDEN LITTLE BROOK

360M RAKES ROCKS

BAREHOLME MOSS

490M

HEY MOSS

280M

300M

OLD QUARRIES

A628

WOODHEAD RESERVOIR

N

YHA

CROWDEN

242M

TORSIDE RESERVOIR

A628

BLACK HILL - 582m
- 450 m of ascent.
- 13 miles / 22 km
- allow 6 hours

Route - Crowden Car Park - Pennine Way - Laddow Rocks - Dun Hill - Black Hill - Sabre F-86 crash site - Swordfish - P4223 - crash site - Black Hill - Tooleyshaw Moss - Sliddens Moss - Gloster Meteors crash site - Tooleyshaw Moor - White Low - Hey Moss - Crowden.

-1:25,000 Outdoor Leisure Map No. 1 - The Dark Peak - West sheet.

- Crowden. Just off the A628 road. Grid Ref. SK072893.

Be self contained. Limited refreshments available at campsite.

ABOUT THE WALK - Renowned for its "boggy" summit and a major obstacle on the Pennine Way. I am pleased that the hand of man has not stretched this far - although you do walk along a stone slab route towards the hill - and the summit area is still a black oozy mass. Unless during a dry summer you still need determination to actually reach the triangulation pillar that now sticks way above the surrounding peat. On my latest visit I had to almost encircle it before finding a "safe" passage to the pillar. The "hill" is aptly named. You will no doubt meet Pennine Wayers on your ascent as they start their second day towards Kirk Yetholm. Choose a fine day for in bad weather the summit is a wild and desolate area. A compass is an essential item, even in fine weather. From the summit you head westwards to the Sabre F-86 crash site and considerable wreckage. You return to Black Hill on bearings to see the Swordfish - P4223 - site. From the hill begin heading southwards back to Crowden with views of Bleaklow and the Longdendale Valley. Part way down you again go on compass bearings to Sliddens Moss to explore the extensive crash site of two Gloster Meteors. You retrace your route back to Tooleyshaw Moor and continue your descent to Crowden.

WALKING INSTRUCTIONS - Exit the car park via its bottom righthand corner, following the signed path to the toilets. Gaining the track beside them turn right and pass the campsite on your left and at the top turn left along the track following the Pennine Way. At the junction the route ahead is your return route. Follow the track over Crowden Brook to a gate and 150 yards later turn right at the path sign - Pennine Way and Black Hill. The path leads to a stile and onto a ladder stile at the boundary of Open Country with a memorial cairn to Harry Phillips, a keen rambler, erected by the Manchester Ramblers in 1980. Continue ascending on the distinct path to the top of Laddow Rocks nearly 1 1/2 miles away. Continue along the top of the rocks with Crowden Great Brook below. The path descends gently to near the brook before ascending gently again. Ahead can be seen the stone slabbed path that curves up the slope of Dun Hill, nearly 2 miles from Laddow Rocks. Beyond the hill you come to a large cairn before walking across the peat to the summit of Black Hill - about 1 3/4 hours of walking from the car park.

From the summit turn eastwards on bearing 63° for 3/4 mile (15 minutes) to Great Hill and the **Sabre F-86** crash site - GR. SK091051. The wreckage is spread over a wide area and is well worth walking around seeing the various fragments. To return to Black Hill first go on bearing 282° for 10 muntes to find the marker post of the **Fairy Swordfish - P4223** - crash site on Heyden Head - GR SK084048. Below in the grough are the remains. Continue to Black Hill on bearing 252°, more than 5 minutes away.

From the summit the direction at first is not obvious because of the flat peat and grough landscape. Go on compass bearing 152° to a stile about 1/4 mile away and once over the pathline becomes more defined and at first is well cairned as you cross Tooleyshaw Moss. You descend gently and about 3/4 mile from the summit - 15 minutes - and before the path ascends gently over Tooleyshaw Moor, turn right on bearing 275° for approximately one mile to the **Gloster Meteors** site - GR. SK069029. You cross easy ground and the wreckage on the grass will be seen from a long distance away. The extensive wreckage is spread over a wide area. Retrace your route back to the slopes of Tooleyshaw Moor and turn right on the ascending path. After the summit - spot height 541m, you descend slightly and ascend White Low - 530m. Here the path turns right and in 1/2 mile gain a large cairn on the edge of the high ground. Descend more steeply taking the "middle" path which soon descends to a track. Keep ahead on the track and pass the large boulders of former quarry activity on your left. Reach a stile on the boundary of Open Country. Descend the path to another stile and track. Turn right to a ladder stile and follow the track to your left to the path junction you passed at the start. Keep straight ahead retracing your steps past the campsite on your right to the toilets and left into the car park.

Fairey Swordfish - P4223 - remains and marker post.

61

North American Sabre - F86 - wreckage near Great Hill.

Glosters Meteor wreckage on Sliddens Moss.

CROWDEN, ARNFIELD CLOUGH & CHEW RESERVOIR - 12 MILES

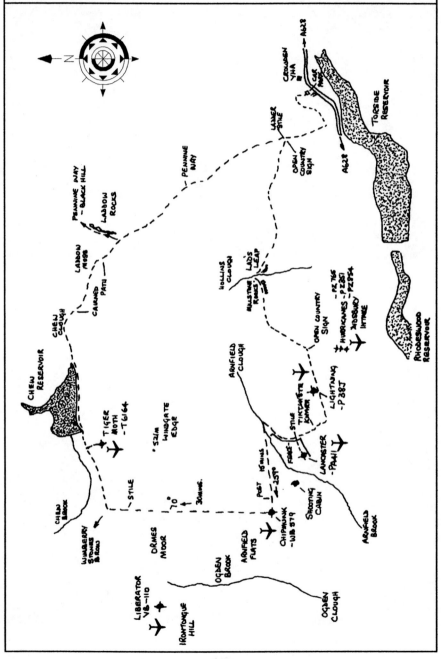

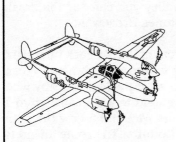

CROWDEN, ARNFIELD CLOUGH & CHEW RESERVOIR - 12 MILES - allow 6 to 7 hours.

Route - Crowden - Pennine Way - Lad's Leap - Millstone Rocks - Lightning P-38J crash site - Tintwistle Knarr - Lancaster PA411 crash site - Arnfield Clough - Chipmunk WB579 crash site - Ormes Moor - Chew Hurdles - Tiger Moth - T6164 crash site - Chew Reservoir - Laddow Rocks - Pennine Way - Crowden.

 - 1:25,000 Outdoor Leisure Map - The Dark Peak No.1 - West Sheet.

 - Crowden. GR SK 023994.

 Refreshments - Limited at Crowden campsite. Basically be self contained.

ABOUT THE WALK - Wonderful remote moorland walk, partly on compass bearing across easy terrain. You follow the start of the Pennine Way section from Crowden and descend it at the end. First you turn westwards onto the southern edge of the Saddleworth Moors to Lad's Leap and on towards Tintwistle Knarr. Here you come to the small remains of the Lighting P-38J close to the path. To the south in Didsbury Intake, three Hurricanes, crashed in flying formation, in 1945; all the wreckage was removed. You continue on the western side of Tintwistle Knarr and onto the remains of a Lancaster - PA411. From here you head north to Arnfield Clough and on a compass bearing head westwards to the small remains of the Chipmunk WB579. Turning north you cross moorland to the head of the Chew Valley; on route westwards is the site of the Liberator VB-110 on Irontongue Hill. The site is on private land and has, alas, been buried. You turn eastwards to Chew Reservoir and deviate a short distance to see the scant remains of the Tiger Moth - T6164 - your last crash site of the day. To return to Crowden you follow a good path to Laddow Rocks and descend the Pennine Way to your earlier path. From the head of the Chew Valley you can see the crash sites detailed in the Dovestone/Wimberry Stones Brow walk.

WALKING INSTRUCTIONS - From the bottom of the car park turn right on a path to the track opposite the campsite and refreshments. Turn right to the top and farm road. Turn left - now on the Pennine Way with the campsite on your left. Follow the track round to a gate and up to a path junction. Turn right, still on the Pennine Way, and follow the path to a stile and onto a ladder stile and Open Country. The route ahead is you return path. Turn left onto a small path and gradually ascend westwards to a wall. Keep it on your left as you ascend and on the "summit" follow it slightly left (westwards) for 1/4 mile to where it turns sharp left. Here bear slightly right, following a cairned path along the moorland edge to Hollins Clough and Coombes Clough at the gritstone boulders of Lad's Leap. Cross the stream and continue along Millstone Rocks and moorland edge for little over 1/4 mile. Where the path turns left and descends gently, turn left and follow it across the heather moorland to a ladder stile and Open Country sign. Do not go over but turn right keeping the fence on your left. Below to your left is the **Hurricanes** crash site. A little over 1/4 mile along the path by the fence, 100 yards to your right can be seen a marker post. Turn right to it and the remains and crash site of the **Lightning P-38J** - GR SK040993.

Continue on the path and where it descends towards Arnfield Brook, turn right - northwards along the gritstone edged Tintwistle Knarr. 1/4 mile from your turning reach the corner of a fence with a gate. Just beyond in a stile. Turn left over this and 150 yards down the gentle slope are the remains of the **Lancaster PA411** - GR SK034994. Armour plating, small cairn and a lot of landing gear can be seen; some of the chrome plating is just like new. Return to the stile and turn left by the fence. This soon swings left and down the slope. Keep to the moorland edge swinging right to Arnfield Clough. Cross the stream at its easy head and cross the moorland on bearing 259° for 15 minutes. The terrain is straight forward peat and should bring you to a large tall wooden post. 100 yards down from here on the northern edge of a grough is a small pile of fragments from the **Chipmunk WB579** - GR SK027997.

Now turn northwards on bearing 70° gently ascending easy moorland, with Ormes Moor and Liberator crash site to your left (west). In more than 20 minutes keep a fence on your left and soon reach a stile and the path from Ormes Moor. Follow it northwards across boggy ground before descending to the cairns and post on the edge of the Chew Valley, at Chew Hurdles. Ahead are stunning views of the valley and Dovestone Reservoir. To your left is the path to Wimberry Stones Brow. Turn right on the path along the edge of the moorland heading towards Chew

Reservoir. In less than 1/2 mile (ten minutes) reach an Open Country sign. Turn right up a shallow cough and in 70 yards take the righthand one and a further 70 yards above it on the right are the handful of remains from the **Tiger Moth - T6164** - GR. SK035016.

Retrace your steps back to the Open Country sign and turn right to Chew Reservoir. Follow the wide path along the righthand side of it. Beyond it cross a footbridge and soon bear right, following the well defined cairned path over Laddow Moss to Laddow Rocks and the Pennine Way, 1/2 mile away. Turn right and descend the Pennine Way following it across Oaken Clough and on beneath Black Tor on your right. 1 1/2 mile from Laddow Rocks you are back at your earlier Ladder Stile. Ascend and retrace your steps along the Pennine Way back to Crowden and the car park.

Aircraft Wrecks seen on this walk -

Lockheed P-38J - Lightning - crashed 10/05/1944 - near Tintwistle Knarr. Small cairn of remains and wooden memorial plaque.

Hawker Hurricanes - PZ765, PZ851. PZ854 - crashed 22/02/1945 - Didsbury Intake. No remains

Avro Lancaster - PA411 - crashed 21/12/1948 - Tintwistle Knarr. Memorial, armour plating and extensive landing gear parts.

De Havilland Canada Chipmunk - WB579 - crashed 03/07/1951 - Arnfield Moor. Small collection of fragments.

Consolidated PB4Y-1 Liberator - VB-110 - crashed 19/12/1943 - crashed Irontongue Hill. Private land and site buried.

De Havilland Tiger Moth - T6164 - crashed 12/04/1945 - Blindstones Moss - a few fragment lying in the peat.

Lockhead P-38J - Lightning crash site and memorial cross.

Avro Lancaster - PA411 - Armour plating and landing struts.

Avro Lancaster - PA411 - propellor gears.

De Havilland Canada Chipmunk - WB579 - remains.

AIRLINER CRASHES ON HILL: 24 DEAD

G-AHCY

3 INJURED: CHILDREN AMONG PASSENGERS

PILOT, OFF COURSE, LOST WAY IN MIST

BOY FOUND STRAPPED IN SEAT ALIVE

FROM OUR SPECIAL CORRESPONDENT

GREENFIELD, YORKS, Friday.

Twenty-four of the 32 occupants of a British European Airways Dakota lost their lives to-day when the plane crashed on a lonely hillside at Kinders Intake, Greenfield, near the Lancashire-Yorkshire border. The remaining eight are all in hospital injured.

Among the dead are the crew of three. Of the 29 passengers, the bodies of eight women, five men and three children have been identified. Two more children, one man and two women were among those named as injured.

The plane was on a flight from Belfast to Manchester. The pilot is believed to have been flying blind in a heavy mist and rain and was off his course when the crash occurred about 1 p.m. Twenty-two people were killed outright and two died in hospital.

The plane hit the 1,200ft hill only a short distance from the summit. With another 50ft of altitude it would have cleared the hill.

The machine burst into ??? and most of the sur???? ??? suffering from ???

PENNINES AIR DISASTER.—The smoking wreckage of the B.E.A.C. Dakota which exploded and burst into flames after crashing into a hillside in Chew Valley, near Oldham, yesterday. The plane, which was flying from Belfast to Manchester, carried 32 people, of whom 24 were killed and eight injured. A rescue party carrying a stretcher can be seen on the skyline. BELOW: Map of the aircraft's route.

Dakota Crash Newspaper cutting - August 1949.
(Dove Stone Moss & Wimberry Stones walk - see next page.)

DOVE STONE MOSS & WIMBERRY STONES - 8 MILES

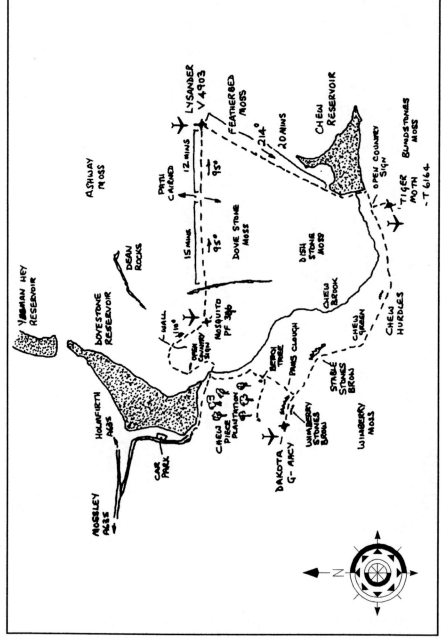

DOVE STONE MOSS
& WIMBERRY STONES
- 8 MILES
- allow 4 to 5 hours.

Route - Dovestone Reservoir Car park - Chew Plantation - Sunny Brow - Mosquito -PF396 crash site - Dove Stone Moss - Featherbed Moss - Lysander V4903 crash site - Chew Reservoir - Tiger Moth - T6164 crash site - Chew Hurdles - Stable Stones Brow - Wimberry Stones Brow - Dakota G-AHCY crash site - Rams Clough - Chew Plantation - Dakota landing gear - Chew Plantation - Dovestone Reservoir.

O.S. MAP

- 1:25,000 Outdoor Leisure Map - No. 1 - The Dark Peak - West sheet.

VISITOR PARKING *- Dovestone Reservoir. GR 014036. off the A635 road.*

- Seasonal refreshments vans in the car park.

ABOUT THE WALK - All the crash sites on this walk have small remains. First you ascend towards Dove Stone Moss to see the Mosquito PF396 crash site. From here you continue on compass bearings across Featherbed Moss to the scant remains of the Lysander V4903. Continuing on bearing you cross easy moorland to Chew Reservoir and the Tiger Moth T6164 crash site just beyond. You now follow a defined path around the southern side of the Chew Valley with impressive views to where you have been walking to Stable Stones Brow and onto Wimberry Stones Brow. Here on August 19th 1949, a Dakota crashed killing 24 passengers; the largest fatalities in the Dark Peak. There is nothing to be seen at the actual crash site. You descend to the bottom of the clough to see the only piece of wreckage remaining, part of the landing gear. From here you soon regain your outward path and return to the car park.

WALKING INSTRUCTIONS - Exit the top end of the car park and follow the track round the reservoir's southern side, past the sailing club to the

73

bridge over Chew Brook - the path to your right is your return route. Follow the wide path round to your left to the eastern side of the reservoir and onto an Open Country sign. Leave the path and bear diagonally right to a gap in the top far righthand corner. Continue with a wall on your right to a gate and stile. Over this keep to the righthand fork between the trees to a gap, boundary wall and open country. Continue on compass bearing 110° and ascend diagonally to your right up the grassy slope. After about 15 minutes reach the base of the rocks beneath Dove Stone Moss. Here you should find the **Mosquito PF396** crash site - GR 024033. A small wall of stones encloses a few remains and a sheet of armoured plating. Ascend steeply (due east) the rocky slope behind to the top and cross a level area before gaining the edge of of Dove Stone Moss. Continue eastwards on bearing 95°, using a clough to the "summit " area of the moorland. Continue on the bearing and 15 minutes from the moorlands edge should cross a cairned path to Chew Reservoir. Continue on your bearing for another 9 minutes to the **Lysander V4903** - GR 041033 - crash site. As you have been crossing this grassy moorland - Featherbed Moss - the Holme Moss TV mast has been in the distance. You route line is to the right of it.

There are only a few pieces of the Lysander to be seen. From the site head south-westerly on bearing 214° for 20 minutes to the western edge of Chew Reservoir. Walk along the grassy path beside it to its end. Turn right, westwards, on a well defined path above Chew Brook. In 300 yards reach an Open Country sign on your left. Turn left up a clough for 70 yards to where it forks. Keep to the righthand one and 70 yards later, above the righthand side of the clough, in a peat area are the few remains of the **Tiger Moth - T6164** - GR SK035016. Retrace your steps back the Open Country sign and edge path and turn left. Follow it to Chew Hurdles more than 1/4 mile away. Continue on the path around the valley with views to Dovestone Reservoir and to where you have walked. Pass Stable Stones Brow and 1/4 mile later just before Wimberry Stones Brow is the steep path down Rams Clough - your route. But first continue onto the impressive Wimberry Stones Brow. Just beyond them is the clough head where the **Dakota G-AHCY** crashed - another 50 feet and it would have cleared the moorland. At the bottom of the clough is a solitary piece of landing gear.

Return to Rams Clough and descend steeply to a solitary beech tree in the top righthand corner of Chew Plantation. Your route is straight ahead but first turn left on a small path, with the plantation wall on your right. Just beyond the western end of the wood gain a gate. Over this bear left into the clough and about 150 yards in it you will find the piece of landing gear. Retrace your steps back to the beech tree and turn left, pass the Oldham Way stile on your left, and descend the path which soon bears left above Chew Brook and on down to your earlier path reached through a gateway. Turn left and follow the track back past the sailing club back to the car park.

Aircraft Wrecks seen on this walk -

De Havilland Mosquito PF396 - crashed south of Dean Rocks - on 22/10/1944. A small enclosure of fragments and piece of armour plating.

Westland Lysander - V4903 - crashed Featherbed Moss - on 19/08/1941. A handful of fragments sticking up from the grassy moorland.

De Havilland Tiger Moth - T6164 - crashed 12/04/1945 - Blindstones Moss - a few fragments lying in the peat.

Douglas Dakota G-AHCY - crashed 19/08/1949 - Wimberry Stones Brow - a solitary piece of landing gear in the clough below the crash site.

TWO OTHER CRASH SITES IN THE SADDLEWORTH AREA -

1. Handley Page Hampden L4055 - crashed 23/05/1940 - Round Hill near Holme - GR. 098058. No remains apart from a bomb crater.
A short walk via Cliff Road (track) from Holme brings you close to the site area.

2. North American Mustang P51D - crashed 29/05/1945 - west of Long Clough, south of Glossop - GR027914. On private land and no remains.
A path from the A624 to Blainsteads Farm passes Long Clough and crash site.

De Havilland Mosquito PF396 - - small enclosure of remains and armour plating.

Westland Lysander - V4903 - fragments.

De Havilland Tiger Moth - T6164 - fragments in the peat..

Douglas Dakota G-AHCY - landing gear.

MARSDEN MOORS - 11 MILES

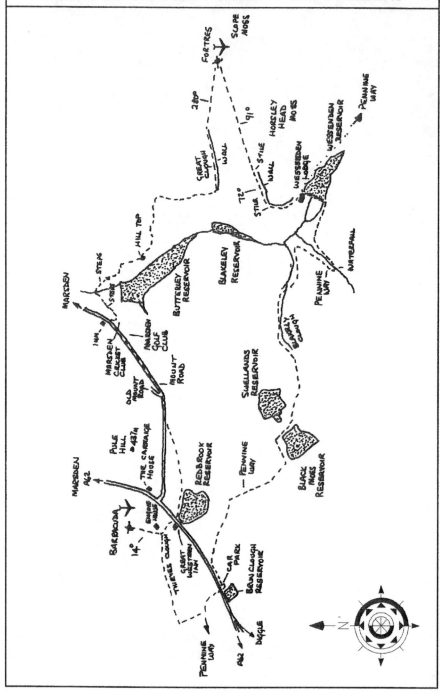

MARSDEN MOORS
- 11 MILES
- allow 5 to 6 hours.

Route - Brunclough Reservoir - Pennine Way - Black Moss Reservoir - Swellands Reservoir - Pennine Way - Blakely Clough - Wessenden Reservoir - Adam Pasture - Horseley Head Moss - Fortress Site, Scope Moss (Meltham Moor) - Great Clough - Scar Head - Butterley Reservoir - Netherley (Marsden) - Mount Road - Redbrook Reservoir - A62 - Thieves Clough - Barracuda Site - Thieves Clough - Pennine Way - Brunclough Reservoir.

Maps - 1:25,000 Outdoor Leisure Maps
- No. 1 - The Dark Peak - West Sheet.
- No. 21 - South Pennines.

Car Park - Beside Brunclough Reservoir, off the A62, where the Pennine Way crosses the road. Grid Ref. SK018095.

Inns - Just off the route in Netherley area of Marsden. The Carriage House, on A62, beneath Pule Hill. Great Western Inn, A62.

ABOUT THE WALK - A walk in the northern extremities of the Dark Peak area of the Peak District National Park, just south of Marsden to see two crash sites. A further site lies to the west in the Castleshaw Valley, but is on private land. First you follow the Pennine Way eastwards to Wessenden Reservoir before going on compass bearings across pleasant moorland to the impressive Fortress site. You return on bearings to the valley above Blakley Reservoir and descend to the northern end of Butterley Reservoir. Here you ascend gradually to Redbrook Reservoir and cross a small section of moorland to the Barracuda site. You ascend the historical Thieves Clough and pick up the Pennine Way for the final 1/4 mile back to Brunclough Reservoir. You pass beneath the impressive craggy summit of Pule Hill, and if time allows you can ascend this noble peak, descending down to The Carriage House Inn.

WALKING INSTRUCTIONS - From the car park pick up the Pennine Way, that heads northeasterly with the A62 road on your left - the opposite side of the road is your return path. Follow the defined path to a stile and enter the Marsden Moor Estate (National Trust property). The path/track swings right with Redbrook Reservoir to your left - you walk beside this near the end of the walk. In 1/2 mile overlooking the reservoir, beside marker post - *MH 720 Yards* - turn right and ascend the stone slabbed path; still on the Pennine Way which you follow to Wessenden Reservoir, three miles away. Ascend a ladder stile and another on the "summit" of the moorland. Continue towards Black Moss Reservoir and turn left, with the reservoir on your right. Walk above its northern side and turn right to walk along its enbankment, with Swellands Reservoir to your left. The path beyond is stone slabbed snaking its way across the moorland and leads you down into Blakely Clough. More than 1/2 mile from the reservoir descend steps and cross to the southern side of Blakely Clough. Follow the path around to your right into another clough with an impressive waterfall at its head. Cross below it and continue on the path on the other side, which leads round to the dam wall of Wessenden Reservoir. Cross to the other side and turn right then left. Here you leave the Pennine Way which turns right here.

Turn left onto a path, with a wall on your left and walk above Wessenden Lodge to a stile. Continue around the field to another stile in the wall with Hey Dike on your right; at Adam Pasture. Turn right and ascend - bearing 72° - up the slope on a small path to stile in top righthand corner and path beside a former conduit; you will follow this later. Go through the stile onto the moorland and begin crossing Horsefield Head Moss on bearing 91°, to the Scope Moss area of Meltham Moor. About 25 minutes of walking will bring you to the **Fortress** crash site - GR071097. Over the crest of relatively easy moorland ahead should be visible on the top of black peat, prominent wreckage of fuselage and undercarriage, partly buried. The surrounding area has many fragments.

From the site head westwards on bearing 280° to a prominent wall, which was to your left as you crossed to the site. Gaining the wall, keep to the righthand side of it, over rough ground, and follow it down to a footbridge over the conduit and stile. Turn right and follow the path for almost 1/2 mile to the head of Rapis Clough, on your left, with Scar Head on your right. Turn left and follow the diagonal descending path to a track head. Follow it for a few yards and before the first house, turn left down to a stile and walled path. Continue along the descending path to a stile and turn right, still on a walled path to a stile and Hill Top house on your left. Here join the house drive and follow it down to a road junction. Turn left descending the road, following round to your right to the track from Butterley Reservoir. Turn left by a path sign and descend the steps down to your right to the bottom of the reservoir slipway. Turn left across the bridge and reach the opposite steps and ascend to the top and a gate. Keep ahead on a path to cricket nets of Marsden Cricket Club. Here gain the club drive and follow it right to Mount Road; with an inn to your right.

Turn left and ascend Mount Road passing Marsden Golf course on your left and right. Pass Forest Farm Bunkhouse on your right and later the junction with Old Mount Road. Continue ahead for 200 yards to a path sign on your left. Follow this path westwards to a footbridge and onto the northern embankment of Redbrook Reservoir. Reach the A62 road opposite the Great Western Inn. Cross to your right to a path and follow to Thieves Clough with notice. You will ascend this path/track - a former Turnpike Road built by Jack Metcalfe (Blind Jack) of Knaesborough in 1759. To your right are the spoil heaps of the Standedge Tunnel of the Huddersfield Narrow Canal. There is also a large Engine House below. Go on compass bearing 14° for about 5 minutes to find the small cairn and remains of the **Barracuda** crash site - GR 024104. Retrace your steps back to Thieves Clough and turn right ascending gently the path and cross Thieves Bridge and continue to where the path forks; keep left to a gate. Continue to another and just after turn left on a track which later curves right to another gate and the Pennine Way. Turn left along the path to the A62 and Brunclough Reservoir.

Aircraft wrecks seen on this walk -

Boeing B-17-G Fortress. Crashed - Meltham Moor - 06/04/1945. - fuselage and landing gear.

Barracuda MD963. Crashed - Redbrook Clough - 19/07/1945 - small cairn and a few fragments.

Three miles west of the route in the Castleshaw Valley - GR. 998107 - and outside the Dark Peak area on private land, are a few remains of a **North American Mustang** - 44-72213. Crashed 30/05/1945.

*Boeing B-17-G Fortress remains on Meltham Moor
- fuselage and landing gear.*

*Barracuda MD963 - Crash site, with Engine House in distance;
small mound of remains.*

SHEFFIELD'S FLYING FORTRESS - "AMIGO MIO"

Strange, I never knew about this one, despite being brought up adjacent to it in Hunter's Bar!

Behind the cafe in Endcliffe Park - Hunter's Bar, Sheffield - is a monument to the crew of the American Airforce B17 Flying Fortress, "Amigo Mio", that crashed here in February 22nd.1944. The plane was on a mission to Denmark but came under attack and was badly damaged. The bombs were dumped in the North Sea and the plane returned to England, not to its base, Chelveston in East Anglia, but towards Sheffield. This is thought because of damaged navigational instruments. Eye witness record the plane came over and the engine noise changed - thought to be one of the engines failing totally from the attack. The plane span out of control and all ten crew were killed.

The pilot, Lt. John Glennon Kriegshauser, from St. Louis, Missouri, USA, was posthumously awarded the Distinguished Flying Cross (D.F.C.). The monument records the names of the ten crew and surrounding the site are ten American oak trees, one for each crew member.

A privately published book about the Flying Fortress - *"Mi Amigo" - The Story of Sheffield's Flying Fortress"* by David Harvey, is available in Sheffield. ISBN 1-901587-00-2.

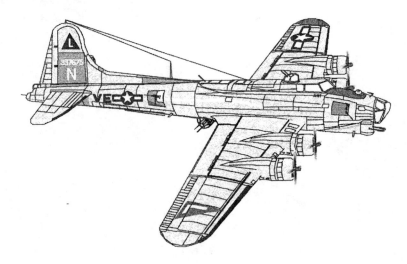

ERECTED BY
SHEFFIELD R.A.F. ASSOCIATION
IN MEMORY OF
THE TEN CREW OF U.S.A.A.F. BOMBER
WHICH CRASHED IN THIS PARK
22-2-1944
PER ARDUA AD ASTRA

AIR CREW
JOHN G. KRIEGHAUSER   HARRY W. ESTABROOKS
LYLE J. CURTIS   CHARLES H. TUTTLE
JOHN W. HUMPHREY   MAURICE O. ROBBINS
MELCHOR HERNANDEZ   VITO R. AMBROSIO
ROBERT E. MAYFIELD   GEORGE U. WILLIAMS

B17 Plaque in Endcliffe Park.

85

PLANE CRASH ANALYSIS -

Total number of planes crashed on moorland of the Dark Peak area of the Peak District (Kinder, Bleaklow, Saddleworth and Marsden Moors) - 57

First crash - July 22nd 1937 - Heyford K6875 - Broadlee Bank Top.

Last crash - December 30th 1963 - Dragon Rapide G-ALBC - Wove Hill, Kinder Scout.

Highest number of a specific plane in one year - 1942 - three of the four crashes were Wellington's.

Highest number in one year - 1945 - 11 crashes.

Busiest period - 1939 - 1945 - (World War 11) - 40 crashes.

Year	no.	Additional comments -
1937	1	First crash
1939	1	
1940	3	Two were Hampden's
1941	8	
1942	4	3 were Wellingtons - all 5 months apart.
1943	6	
1944	7	2 were Liberators. Includes V1 Rocket.
1945	11	2 Oxford's. 3 Hurricanes - 22/11/45.
1948	2	
1949	1	
1950	1	
1951	4	2 were Meteors. 2 independent crashes on same day - April 12th. 1951.
1952	2	
1954	3	2 Sabres - Ashop Moor.
1956	1	
1957	1	
1963	1	

Year list - 1939 - 1963 - of Aircraft wrecks on Kinder, Bleaklow, Saddleworth & Marsden Moors -

1939
Blenheim L1476 - Sykes Moor. - 30/1/39

1940
Swordfish P4223 - Heyden Head. - 25/1/40
Hampden X3154 - North of Chapel en le Frith - 21/12/40
Hampden L4055 - Holmfirth - 23/5/40

1941
Botha W5103 - Round Hill - 10/12/41
Defiant N3378 - Nr Bleaklow Stones - 29/8/41
Blenheim 1V - Crowden Tower - 3/7/41
Blenheim Z5746 - Ox Stones - 26/1/41
Defiant N1766 - Rowlee Pastures - 12/4/41
Wellington W5719 - Upper Tor - 31/7/41
Lyrander V9403 - Slate Pit Moss - 19/8/41
Anson N9912 - Whitwell Moor - 31/3/41

1942
Hampden AE381 - Cluther Rocks - 21/1/42
Wellington Z8491 - White Edge Moor - 6/2/42
Wellington Z8980 - Rudd Hill - 17/7/42
Wellington DU810 - Broomhead Moor - 9/12/42

1943
Wellington X3348 - Blackden Edge - 26/1/43
Thunderbolt P47C - Homehill Tor - 25/4/43
Liberator PB47 - Broken Ground - 18/12/43
Liberator - VB-110 - Irontoungue Hill - 19/12/43
Spitfire PZ883 - Rushup Edge - 10/12/43
Halifax HR727 - Blackden Edge - 5/10/43
Oxford LX518 - Margery Hill - 19/10/43

1944
Lightning P38J - Tintwistle Knarr - 10/5/44
Liberator B24H -20 - Twiggle Head Moss - 9/10/44
Mosquito PF395 - Dean Rocks - 22/10/44
Liberator B24J - Mill Hill - 11/10/44
Stirling LJ628 - Upper Commans - 21/7/44
Anson N9853 - Edale Moor - 11/12/44
V1 Flying bomb - Cut Gate - 24/12/44

1945
Lancaster - James Thorn - 18/5/45
C47 - Shelf Moor - 24/7/45
3 Hurricans PZ851, PZ765, PZ854 - Didsbury Intake - 22/11/45
Fortress B-17G-65 - Meltham Moors - 6/4/45
Anson NL185 - The Cloughs - 23/11/45
Oxford HN594 - Brown Knoll - 28/12/45
Oxford NM683 - Rushup Edge - 4/3/45
Tiger Moth T6164 - Chew Brook - 12/4/45
Barracuda MD963 - Redbrook Clough - 29/7/45

1948
Superfortress RB29A - High Shelf Stone - 3/11/48
Lancaster PA411 - Rhodes Hill - 20/12/48

1949
Dakota G-AHCY - Wimberry Stones - 19/8/49

1950
Meteor RA487 - Hagg Side - 8/12/50

1951
Chipmunk WB579 - Arnfield Moor - 3/7/51
2 Meteors WA971, VZ518 - Shiddens Moor - 12/4/51
Consul TF-RPM - Crow Stone Edge - 12/4/51

1952
Harvard FT415 - Wool Packs - 14/1/52
Wellington MF627 - Ughill - 17/10/52

1954
Sabre F86E - Black Hill - 14/12/54
2 Sabre XD707 & XD730 - Ashop Moor - 22/7/54

1956
L. 20A Beaver - Bramah Edge - 5/12/56

1957
Miles Hawk Q-AJSF - Kinderlow End - 29/7/57

1963
Dragon Rapide G-ALBC - Kinder Scout - 30/12/63

Some brief facts about the planes -

1. AIRSPEED OXFORD -
Three-seat advanced trainer. Wooden structure, plywood- covered. The RAF's first twin engined monoplane trainer. Started in use in November 1937; over 8,700 built.
Maker's Designation - AS10 (Oxford I and II); AS46 (Oxford V).
Manufacturers - Airspeed (1934) Ltd, Portsmouth and Christchurch. Sub-contracted by D.H.,Stndard and Percival.
Engine - Mk II: Two 370hp Armstrong Siddeley Cheetah X.
 - Mk V: Two 450hp Pratt & Whitney Wasp Junior.
Dimensions - Span, 53ft 4in; length, 34ft 6in; height 11ft 1 in; wing area, 348sq ft.
Weights - Mk II: Empty, 5,380lb; loaded, 7,600lb. Mk V: Empty, 5670lb; loaded, 8,000lb.
Performance - Mk II: Max speed,188mph; climb, 960ft / min; service ceiling, 19,500ft.
MK V: Max speed, 202 mph; climb, 2,000ft/min; service ceiling, 21,000ft.

2. AVRO ANSON Mk 1 (N9912) -
UK built from 1934 - 1952. Primarily as a light transport or coastal reconnaisance plane. Known as the "faithfull Annie". More than 11,000 were built.
Engine - two 355 hp Armstrong Siddeley Cheetah 1X
Max speed - 188 mph (302.5 km)
Ceiling - 19,000 ft. (5,790m)
Range - 1,271 km.
Weight - Empty - 5375 lbs (2,438 kg)
Arnaments - Max of 4 - 0.303 machine gun.
Dimension - Wingspan - 56'-6" (17.22m)
Length - 42 ft 3in (12.88 m)
Height - 3.99m) 13ft 1 in.

3.FAIREY BARRACUDA (1943-1953) -

Torpedo bomber Reconaissance design with provision made for a single torpedo or 1,500lbs of bombs, depth charges or arms. Prototype flown (P1767) on 7th December 1940.

Arnament - 1 or 2 rear mounted 303 in machine gune.

Crew - 3

Engine - Rolls Royce Merlin engine.

Mark I - out of service by 1946 - 30 built.

Mark II - more powerful Merlin Engine - 1,688 made.

Mark III - 852 made.

'In service the Barracuda proved difficult to fly and early casualties included crews used to slow byplane".

Speed MK I - 221 mph. MK II - 228 mph

Weight - Mk I - 12,065 lbs. MK II - 12,600 lbs

From 1945 used for training.

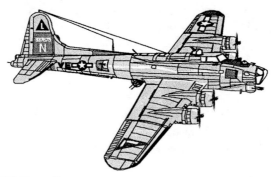

4. BOEING B - 17G Flying Fortess. -

USA - 10 Crew heavy bomber.

Engine - 4 - 1,200hp Wright R-1820 - 97 nine cylinder radial engines.

Max speed - 302mph (486km)

Range - 1,800 miles (2,897km)

Weight - empty - 44,560lbs (20,212kg)

          Max - 72,000lbs (32,659kg)

Wingspan - 103ft 0" (31.63m)
Length - 74ft 9" (22.78m)
Height - 19ft 1" (5.82m)
Armaments - 13 overall - 2 -0.5" machine guns Chin turret
1 - 0.5" machine gun in each check position,
2 - 0.5" machine gun Dorsal turret.
1 - 0.5" machine guns in roof position.
2 - 0.5" machine guns Ventral position
2 - 0.5" machine guns tail
1 - 0.5" machine guns in each waist position.

Bomb load 17,600lbs (7983kg).

5. BOULTON PAUL DEFIANT -
Powered by one 1,030 hp Rolls Royce Merlin 111 engine.
Wing span - 39' 4"
Length - 35' 4"
Max speed - 303 mph at 16,500 ft.
Armaments - 4 .303 Browning in power-op turret.

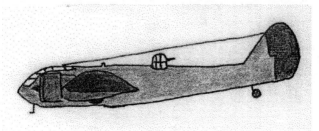

6. BRISTOL BLENHEIM MK1 -
UK Light 3 seater bomber of WWII.
2 - Engines - 840hp Bristol Mercury VIII nine cylinder single row radial engines.
Max speed - 285mph (459km)
Range - 1,125 mile (1810km)
Weight - empty - 8,839 lbs (4,013kg)
            max - 13,100lbs (5,947kg)
Wingspan - 56ft 4" (17.17m)
Length - 39ft 9" (12.12m)
Height - 9ft 10" (3m)

Arnaments - 1,000lb (454kg) bomb load.
1 -0.303 machine gun on Port wing
1 - 0.30 machine gun dorsal turret.

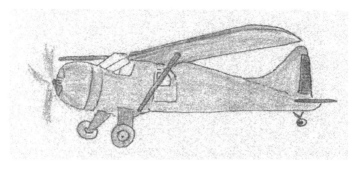

7. CANADA BEAVER (De HAVILLAND) -1961 -1988.
Originally flown in 1947
Army Aviation - for liaison flying and training
Crew -   2 crew & 4 passengers
Range - 100 miles
Became retired in 1989
Engine - Wasp R985
Speed - 160mph.
Weight - 5,100 lb
Number - 42.

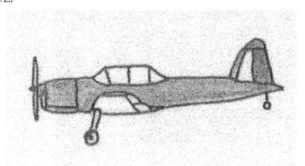

8. de HAVILLAND CHIPMUNK T MK 10 -
Two-seat elementary trainer. All metal stressed-skin constuction.
Maker's designation: DHC.1.
Manufacturer - de Havilland Aircraft Co. Ltd, Hatfield, Herts, and Chester.
Engine   - One 145 hp de Havilland Gipsy Major 8.
Dimensions   - Span, 34ft 4in; length, 25ft 8 in; height. 7ft 1in; wing area, 172sq ft.
Weights   - Empty, 1,417lb; loaded, 2,000lb.
Performance - Max speed, 138mph at sea level; cruising speed, 119mph; Initial climb,
800ft/min, and 7.3 min to 5,000ft; range, 300 miles endurance, 2.3 hours; service
ceiling, 16,000ft.

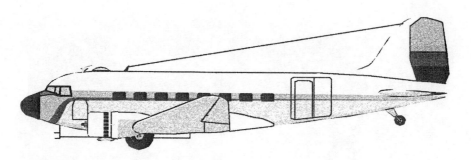

9. DOUGLAS C-47 SKYTRAIN/DAKOTA -

More than 10,000 of these USA Transporter planes were built. Two or three crew
with room for 28 troops or 10,000 lb (4,536 kg) of freight.
Engine - 2 - 1,200 hp Pratt & Whitney - R-1830-92 - 14 cylinder two row radical
engine.
Max speed - 230 mph (370 km)
Range - 1,600 mile (2,575 km)
Weight empty - 17,865 lb (8,103kg)
Wingspan - 95ft (28.90m)
Length - 64ft 51/2" - (19.63m)
Height - 16ft 11" - (5.20m)

10. DRAGON RAPIDE -

(Dominie I) Five - or six-seat radior or navigation trainer (MkI) or ten-seat
communications aircraft (Mk II). Wooden structure, fabric covered.
Maker's designation: DH 89A.
Manufacturers - de Havilland Aircraft Co.Ltd, Hatfield, Herts. Sub-contracted by
Bush Coachworks, Loughborough, Leics.
Engine -   Two 200hp de Havilland Gipsy Queen.
Dimension - Span, 48ft; length, 34ft 6in; height, 10ft 3in; wing area, 340sq ft.
Weights - Empty, 3,230lb; loaded, 5,500lb.
Performance - Max speed, 157mph at 1,000ft, cruising speed, 132mph,
initial climb, 867ft/min; range, 570 miles, service ceiling, 16,700ft.

11. FAIREY SWORDFISH MKI -
UK 3 seater torpedo bomber and level bomber biplane. At the start of WWII there were 13 operational Swordfish sqdns. 989 were built.
Engine - 1 - 775hp Bristol Regasus 111M3 nine cylinder single row radial engine.
Max speed - 139mph (224km)
Range - 1,030 miles (1657km)
Weight - empty 5,200lbs (2,359kg) max - 9,250lbs (4,196kg)
Wingspan - 45ft 6" (13.87m)
Length - 36ft 4" (11.07m)
Height - 13ft 53/4" (4.11m)
Arnaments - 1 - 0.303 machine starboard side of forward fuselage
 - 1 - 0.303 - near cockpit.
External bomb load - 1,600lb (726kg)

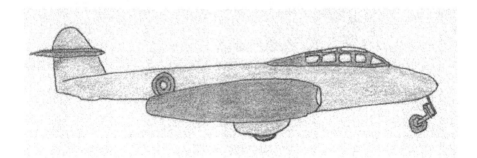

12. GLOSTERS METEOR -
- Early gas turbine and became a very successful jet fighter.
Engine - ME TROVIAL F.2. BERYL turbojet, first run in Dec. 1941.
Used to power Twin-jet in Nov. 1943.
- Used against VI in July 1944.
- The only Allied jet aircraft to be operational in WW II.
- First sqd to fly during the war the 616.

Later.
2 - RR Derwent & Turbojet.
Engine - 3,500lb thrust.
Crew   - 1
Max Speed - 598mph (962km) at 33,000lb (10,000m)
Range -   980 miles (1,580km)
Ceiling -   43,000ft (13,106m)
Length -   44 ft 7in (13.58m)
Height   -   13ft (3.96m)
Span   -   37ft 2in (11.32m)
By July 1961 - 3,850 built in UK.

13. HANDLEY PAGE HALIFAX -
A Major RAF heavy seven seat bomber during the second part of WWII. Cost about
£50,000 in 1943
4-1,615 hp - Binnlot Hercules VI Engines.
Max speed - 282 mph (454 km)
Range - 1,985 miles - (3,194 km) with 7,000lb (3,175 kg) bomb load. (Internal bomb
laod 14,700 lbs - (6,577 kg)
Weight empty - 42,500 lbs - (19,278 kg) Max - 65,000 lbs - (29,484 kg).
Wingspan - 98ft 8" - (30.07m)
Length - 71ft 4"- (21.74m)
Height - 20ft 1" - (6.12m)
Arnaments - Nose turret - 1 - 0.303 machine gun. Dorsal turret - 4 - 0.303 machine
gun.

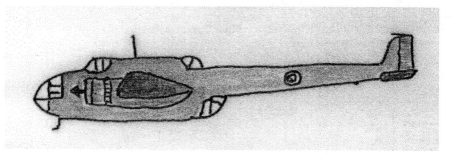

14. HANDLEY PAGE HAMPDEN –
UK 4 seater medium bomber.
2 – 1,000hp Bristol Regasus XVIII nine – cylinder singe row radial engines.
Max speed – 255 mph (426km)
Range – 1,885 mies (3,034 km) with 2,000lb – (907kg) bomb load.
Weight empty – 11,780lbs (5343kg)
Max – 22,500lbs (10,206kg)
Wingspan – 69ft 2" (21.08m)
Length – 53ft 7" (16.33m)
Height – 14ft 11" (4.55m)
Arnaments – Bomb load 4000lbs (1814kg)
6 machine guns – 0.303. – 1 part side of foreward findage, 1 in nose, 2 in dorsal and 2 in ventral position.

15. HANDLEY PAGE HEYFORD Mks I to III –
(Heyford IA) Heavy night bomber with a crew of four. Metal construction, fabric covered.
Maker's designation: HP 50.
Manufacturer – Handley Page Ltd, Cricklewood, London. NW2.
Engine – Two 575hp Rolls-Royce Kestrel IIIS.
Dimensions – Span, 75ft; length, 58ft; height, 17ft 6in; wing area, 1,470 sq ft.
Weights – Empty, 9,200lb; loaded, 16,900lb.
Performance – Max speed, 142mph at 13,000ft; climb, 15.3 min to 10,000ft; range, 920 miles with 1,600lb bomb load; service ceiling, 21,000ft

Arnament - Three Lewis guns in nose and midships position and vental 'dustbin'. Bomb load, 2,000lb (2,660lb in Mk III).
Squadron Allocations - Home Bomber: Nos 7 (Worthy Down and Finningley), 9 (Aldergrove, Scampton and Stradishall), 10 and 78 (Boscombe Down and Dishforth), 38 (Mildenhall and Marham), 97 and 166 (Boscombe Down and Dishforth), 99 (Upper Heyford and Mildenhall), 102 (Worthy Down, Finningley, Honington and Driffield). 148 (Stradishall) and 149 (Mildenhall).

16. NORTH AMERICAN AT-6 HARVARD (Texan)
Country of origin   -   USA. Cheap trainer plane with handling characteristics of a fighter plane. About 15,000 were built. First flight in April 1936 and used until 1955.

Engines - Pratt & Whitney R-1340-49 Wasp 9- cylinder radial, air cooled, 600 hp.
Crew -   two
Max Speed - 208mph (335 km/h)
Range - 750 miles (1,025 km)
Ceiling - 24,200ft (7,325m)
Length - 29ft 0in (8.84m)
Span - 42ft 0in (12.80m)
Height - 11ft 9in (3.55m)

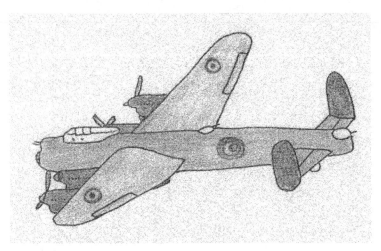

17. AVRO 683 LANCASTER

County of origin UK. 7,377 made between October 1941 - 1946. Originally designed as the Avro Manchester 111 in 1939 but was soon renamed the Lancaster and primarily used as night bomber.

Crew - Seven.
Engines - four 1,460hp Rolls-Royce Merlin XX cooled inline.
Max speed - 275 m.p.h. at 15,000 ft (fully loaded)
Cruising speed - 200 mph at 15,000 ft.
- 245 mph at sea ;level.
Range - 2,530 miles (7,000 lb load)
- 1,730 miles (12,000 lb load)
- 1,550 miles (22,000 lb load)
Service ceiling height - 19,000 ft.
Armaments -
- Nose turret - 2 .303 machine guns.
- Tail turret - 4 .303 machine guns.
Wingspan - 102' (31.1m.)
Length - 69' 6" (21.2m)
Height - 20ft 0in (6.10 m)
Weight - 65,000 lbs
Bomb load - initially 8,000 lbs but modified to 22,000 lbs.

Bomb load - 4,000 lbs (1,818 kg). Later modified to carry 22,000lb (10,000kg) Grand Slam bomb designed by Dr. Barnes Wallis. The plane became famous for its use in the 617 Dambusters Squadron.

The Lancaster served from January 1942 in 54 squadrons. Between them they dropped over 60% of Bomber Command tonnage throughput the war. Nearly 4,000 were lost, mainly in action. Out of a total of 32 V.C.'s awarded nine were awarded to Lancaster crews.

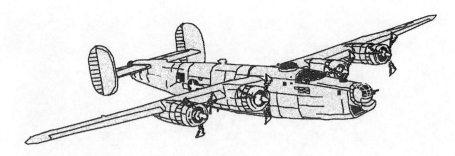

18. CONSOLIDATED PB4Y LIBERATOR -

US Navy Anti submarine squadron, operating out of Dunkeswell, Devon, with a crew of between 8 - 12.

Engines - 4 - 1,200hp Pratt & Whitney R -1830-65 14 cylinder two nose radical engine.

Max speed - 300 mph (483 km)

Range - 2,100 miles (3,380 km)

Weight empty - 36,500 lbs (16,556 kg)

       Max - 65,000 lbs (29,484 kg).

Wingspan - 110 ft - (33.53m)

Length - 67 ft 2" - (20.47m)

Height - 18 ft - (5.49m)

Arnaments - Could carry upto 8,800 bomb load. 2 - machine guns in nose, dorsal and tail turrets. 2 machine guns in waist positions.

19. WESTLAND LYSANDER -

UK's main reconaissance plane.

1 Engine - 890hp Bristol Mercury XII nine cylinder single radial engine

Max speed - 229 mph (369 km)

Range - 600 miles (966 km)

Weight empty - 4,065 lb (1,855 kg)

Wingspan - 50ft (15,24m)

Length - 30'-6" (9,30m)

Height - 11ft (3.35m)

Arnament - 2 - 0.303 machine guns in wheel fairings.

Further machine gun in rear cockpit.

20. MILES HAWK -
M2 Hawk - 2 seater light touring aircraft - first flown on 29 March 1933.
powered by -   De Havilland Gipsy engines.
The Hawk trainer - almost 1,300 built for flying clubs.

21. De HAVILLAND MOSQUITO -
A Most successful UK RAF Light Bomber. The two seater MK XVI had an enlarged
bomb bay to take a 4,000 lb blast bomb. (Dean Rocks, Chew Valley, 22/10/1944 - this
one was returning from a raid on Hamburg -)
2 Engines 1,680 hp Rolls Royce Merlin. 72/73.
Max speed - 415 mph (668 km)
Range - 1,795 miles (2,888 km) with a 2,000 lb (907kg) bomb.
Weight - empty - 15,500 lbs (7,031 kg)
Wingspan - 54ft 2" (16.51m)
Length - 44ft 6" (13.56m)
Height - 15ft 3" (4.65m)
No Arnaments as the plane was believed to be so effective and operational that none
was required.

22. NORTH AMERICAN P51D MUSTANG -
A major single seater fighter plane of WWII.
1 Engine - 1,695 hp Puckered V-1650 - 7 - 12 cylinder V engine.
Max speed - 437 mph (703 km) could climb to 20,000 ft in 7 mins 18 secs.
Range - 2,301 miles (3,703 km)
Weight empty - 6,840 lbs (3,103kg)
Wingspan - 37 ft - 0.25" (11.28 m)
Length - 32 ft - 3.025" (9.84 m)
Height - 13ft 8" (4.16m)
Arnaments - 6 - 0.5" fixed forward firing machine guns on front edge of wings.

23. NORTH AMERICAN F-86 SABRE -
Country of Origin - USA. Used in Korean War. The first swept wing fighter. In front line
use for 20 years.
Engines - General Electric J47-GE-17B turbojet, 7,500lb (3,402kg) thrust.
Crew - one
Max speed - 692mph (1,113 km/h)
Range - 850 miles (1,378 km)
Ceiling - 50,000ft (15,240 m)
Length - 40ft 11in (12.47m)
Span - 39ft 1in (11.91m)
Height - 14ft 8in (4.47m).

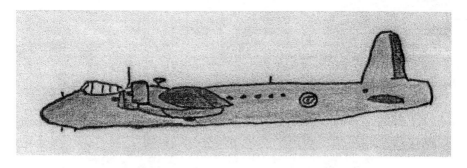

24. SHORT STIRLING LJ628 -

The first UK 4 engined heavy duty bomber in Bomber Command in WWII.
2,374 produced.

Crew 7 -8

4 Engines - 1,650 hp Bristol Hercules XV1 - 14 cylinder 2- ton radial engines.

Max speed - 270 mph (434 km)

Range - 2,010 miles (3,235) km with 3,500 lb
(1,588kg) bomb load.

Weight - empty - 46,900 lbs (21,274 kg)
          - max - 70,000lbs (31,752 kg)

Wingspan - 99ft 1" (30.20m)

Length - 87ft 3" (26.59m)

Height - 22ft 9" (6.93m)

Arnaments:- 14,000lbs (6350kg) bomb load
           - 2- 0.303 machine gun in nose turret & dorsal turret
           - 4- 0.303 machine gun in tail

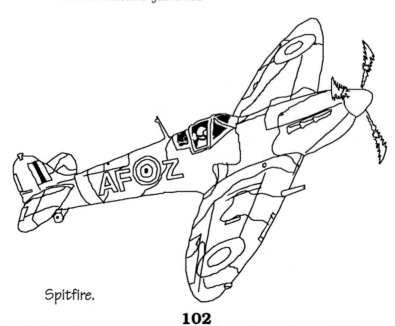

Spitfire.

25. SUPERMARINE SPITFIRE -

BRITISH MADE FROM 1937. SINGLE ENGINE MONOPLANE. THE BEST KNOWN SINGLE-SEAT FIGHTER PLANE OF WORLD WAR 1L DESIGNED BY REGINALD MITCHELL OF HANLEY, STOKE ON TRENT. THERE IS A MONUMENT TO HIM THERE. IT WAS THE FIRST ALL METAL BRITISH FIGHTER AND WAS USED BY THE RAF FROM 1938 ONWARDS. THE ENGINE ON THE MK 1A WAS A ROLLS ROYCE MERLIN - MORE THAN 1,030 HP - AND DESIGNED BY ARTHUR RUBBRA - A GREAT FRIEND OF MY LATE FATHER. THE PLANE SAW MAJOR ACTION IN THE BATTLE OF BRITAIN, 1940. THE WINGS WERE ARMED WITH EIGHT .303 BROWNING MACHINE GUNS. IN 1946 THE MK24 WAS BROUGHT INTO SERVICE TOGETHER WITH A SEAFIRE, FOR USE FROM AIRCRAFT CARRIERS.

MAX SPEED - 367 M.P.H. (591KM).
WINGSPAN - 36' 10" (11.3M)
LENGTH - 29' 11' (9.1M).
CEILING HEIGHT - 37,000 FT.
RATE OF CLIMB - 2,666 FT PER MINUTE.
RANGE - 470 MILES
WEIGHT - 7,500 LBS.

26. DE HAVILLAND D.H. 82 TIGER MOTH -

COUNTRY OF ORIGIN - UK. USED BY THE RAF FROM FEBUARY 1932 AND BECAME THE INITIAL TRAINING PLANE OF WW1L ABOUT 4,000 USED BETWEEN 1932 - 1947.
ENGINES - ONE 130 HP DE HAVILLAND GYPSY MAJOR AIR-COOLED INLINE.
CREW - TWO.
MAX SPEED - 109MPH (176 KM/H)
RANGE - 300 MILES (482 KM)
CEILING - 14,000 FT (4,267 KM)
LENGTH -   23 FT 11IN (7.29 M)
SPAN - 29FT 4IN (8.94M)
HEIGHT - 8FT 9.5IN (2.66M)

27. REPUBLIC THUNDERBOLT P47C -
USA single seater fighter plan - 602 made.
1 Engine - 2,000 hp R - 2800.21 Pratt & Whitney Engine.
Max speed - 435 mph (700 km)
Range - 1,725 miles (2776 km)
Weight empty - 10,700 lbs (4858 kg)
Wingspan - 40 ft 9" (12.42 m)
Length - 36 ft 1" (10.99m)
Height - 14ft 7" (4.44m)
Arnaments - 8 - 0.5" machine guns on front wings.

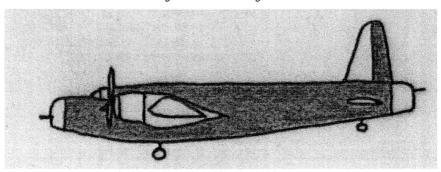

28. THE VICKERS WELLINGTON BOMBER -
British made and dates from 1940 and used as a long range bomber, primarily on night raids.
Powered by two 1,000 hp British Pegasus XVIII engines.
Max speed - 235m.p.h. (378km). at 15,500 ft.
Rate of climb - 1,120 feet per minute.
Ceiling height - 18,000 feet.
Range - 1,200 miles.
Wingspan - 86' 2" (26.3m.)
Length - 64' 7" (19.7m.)
Armaments -
Nose turret - 2 .303 machine guns
Tail Turret - 2 .303 machine guns.

29. LOCKHEED LIGHTNING P38J –
USA single seater long range bomber; 2,970 of the 38J were built. Armaments, fixed in nose.
Weight – 12,800lbs empty. Max – 21,600lbs.
Engines – 2 – 1,600 h.p. Allison 12 cylinder.
Max speed – 414 mph (666km/h.
Range – 2,600 miles (4,184 km.)
Ceiling – 44,000ft (13,400m).
Lenght – 37ft 10" (11.53m)
Span – 52ft. (15.85m)
Height – 12ft 10" (3.91m)

30. V-1 Flying Bomb (Buzz bomb) –
Pioletless aircraft launched from sites around Calais in France from June 1944. Eventually
more than 8,000 were launched on London. Preset flight distance; when engine ceased
plummeted to earth and bomb exploded.
Powered by a pulse-jet engine with a range of 150 miles (240km.)
Length – 25.9 ft (7.9m).
Wingspan – 17.3 ft (5.3m).
Weight – 4,806 lbs (2,180 kg).
Speed – 350 to 400 mph (563 to 644 km.p.h.)

WALK RECORD CHART

KINDER AREA -

Kinder Low and Rushup Edge - 10 miles ....

Blackden Edge and Grindsbrook Knoll - 6 miles ....

Snake Path - 12 miles ....

BLEAKLOW AREA -

Higher Shelf Stones - 5 miles ....

Bleaklow Head - 15 miles ....

Margery Hill and Outer Edge - 12 miles ....

Broomhead Moor and Whitwell Moors - 3 and 5 miles ....

CHEW AND MARSDEN MOOR AREA

Black Hill - 14 miles ....

Crowden, Arnfield Clough & Chew Reservoir - 12 miles ....

Dove Stone Moss & Wimberry Stones - 8 miles ....

Marsden Moors - 11 miles ....

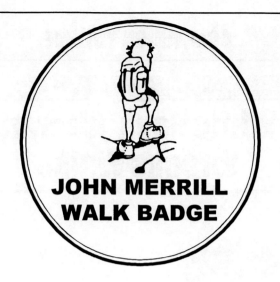

JOHN MERRILL WALK BADGE

THE JOHN MERRILL WALK BADGE

Complete six walks in this book and get the above special embroidered badge and signed certificate. Badges are Blue cloth with lettering and hiker embroidered in four colours.

BADGE ORDER FORM

Date walks completed...

NAME ....

ADDRESS ....

....

Price: £4.50 each including postage, packing, VAT and signed completion certificate. Amount enclosed (Payable to Walk & Write Ltd) ..
From: Walk & Write Ltd.,
Marathon House, Longcliffe,
Nr. Matlock, Derbyshire. DE4 4HN

Tel /Fax 01629 - 540991
*********** YOU MAY PHOTOCOPY THIS FORM ***********

"HAPPY WALKING!" T SHIRT
- Yellow (daisy) with black lettering and walking man logo.
Send £8.95 to Walk & Write Ltd., stating size required.
Happy walking embroidered, full length zipped, Fleece Jacket - £17.95

COMPANION VOLUME

AIRCRAFT WRECK WALKS SERIES

White Peak Aircraft Wrecks Walks

WHITE PEAK AIRCRAFT WRECK WALKS by John N. Merrill

Bristol Fighter MK111 - crashed Matlock Moor, July 16th. 1928.

by John N. Merrill

Scattered around the hills and dales of the White Peak and Derbyshire are the locations of where more than twenty military planes came down. These short circular walks - 4 to 8 miles long - take you on the nearest right of way to the sites and monuments. One final walk - The Dam Busters Walk - takes you around Derwent and Howden Reservoirs where practice flights for that daring raid were carried out. New enlarged edition with details of more than fifty crash sites in the White Peak and southern half of Derbyshire.
...........Happy Walking!

OTHER JOHN MERRILL WALK BOOKS

CIRCULAR WALK GUIDES -
SHORT CIRCULAR WALKS IN THE PEAK DISTRICT - Vol. 1,2 and 3
CIRCULAR WALKS IN WESTERN PEAKLAND
SHORT CIRCULAR WALKS IN THE STAFFORDSHIRE MOORLANDS
SHORT CIRCULAR WALKS - TOWNS & VILLAGES OF THE PEAK DISTRICT
SHORT CIRCULAR WALKS AROUND MATLOCK
SHORT CIRCULAR WALKS IN "PEAK PRACTICE COUNTRY."
SHORT CIRCULAR WALKS IN THE DUKERIES
SHORT CIRCULAR WALKS IN SOUTH YORKSHIRE
SHORT CIRCULAR WALKS IN SOUTH DERBYSHIRE
SHORT CIRCULAR WALKS AROUND BUXTON
SHORT CIRCULAR WALKS AROUND WIRKSWORTH
SHORT CIRCULAR WALKS IN THE HOPE VALLEY
40 SHORT CIRCULAR WALKS IN THE PEAK DISTRICT
CIRCULAR WALKS ON KINDER & BLEAKLOW
SHORT CIRCULAR WALKS IN SOUTH NOTTINGHAMSHIRE
SHORT CIRCULAR WALKS IN CHESHIRE
SHORT CIRCULAR WALKS IN WEST YORKSHIRE
WHITE PEAK DISTRICT AIRCRAFT WRECKS
CIRCULAR WALKS IN THE DERBYSHIRE DALES
SHORT CIRCULAR WALKS FROM BAKEWELL
SHORT CIRCULAR WALKS IN LATHKILL DALE
CIRCULAR WALKS IN THE WHITE PEAK
SHORT CIRCULAR WALKS IN EAST DEVON
SHORT CIRCULAR WALKS AROUND HARROGATE
SHORT CIRCULAR WALKS IN CHARNWOOD FOREST
SHORT CIRCULAR WALKS AROUND CHESTERFIELD
SHORT CIRCULAR WALKS IN THE YORKS DALES - Vol 1 - Southern area.
SHORT CIRCULAR WALKS IN THE AMBER VALLEY (Derbyshire)
SHORT CIRCULAR WALKS IN THE LAKE DISTRICT
SHORT CIRCULAR WALKS IN THE NORTH YORKSHIRE MOORS
SHORT CIRCULAR WALKS IN EAST STAFFORDSHIRE
DRIVING TO WALK - 16 Short Circular walks south of London by Dr. Simon Archer Vol 1 and 2
LONG CIRCULAR WALKS IN THE PEAK DISTRICT - Vol.1,2 ,3 and 4.
DARK PEAK AIRCRAFT WRECK WALKS
LONG CIRCULAR WALKS IN THE STAFFORDSHIRE MOORLANDS
LONG CIRCULAR WALKS IN CHESHIRE
WALKING THE TISSINGTON TRAIL
WALKING THE HIGH PEAK TRAIL
WALKING THE MONSAL TRAIL & OTHER DERBYSHIRE TRAILS
PEAK DISTRICT WALKING - TEN "TEN MILER'S" - Vol One and Two
CLIMB THE PEAKS OF THE PEAK DISTRICT
PEAK DISTRICT WALK A MONTH Vols One,Two, Three, and Four
TRAIN TO WALK Vol. One - The Hope Valley Line
DERBYSHIRE LOST VILLAGE WALKS -Vol One and Two.
CIRCULAR WALKS IN DOVEDALE AND THE MANIFOLD VALLEY
CIRCULAR WALKS AROUND GLOSSOP
WALKING THE LONGDENDALE TRAIL
WALKING THE UPPER DON TRAIL
SHORT CIRCULAR WALKS IN CANNOCK CHASE
CIRCULAR WALKS IN THE DERWENT VALLEY
WALKING THE TRAILS OF NORTH-EAST DERBYSHIRE

CANAL WALKS -
VOL 1 - DERBYSHIRE & NOTTINGHAMSHIRE
VOL 2 - CHESHIRE & STAFFORDSHIRE
VOL 3 - STAFFORDSHIRE
VOL 4 - THE CHESHIRE RING
VOL 5 - LINCOLNSHIRE & NOTTINGHAMSHIRE
VOL 6 - SOUTH YORKSHIRE
VOL 7 - THE TRENT & MERSEY CANAL
VOL 8 - WALKING THE DERBY CANAL RING
VOL 9 - WALKING THE LLANGOLLEN CANAL
VOL 10 - CIRCULAR WALKS ON THE CHESTERFIELD CANAL
VOL 11 - CIRCULAR WALKS ON THE CROMFORD CANAL

JOHN MERRILL DAY CHALLENGE WALKS -
WHITE PEAK CHALLENGE WALK
THE HAPPY HIKER - WHITE PEAK - CHALLENGE WALK No.2
DARK PEAK CHALLENGE WALK
PEAK DISTRICT END TO END WALKS
STAFFORDSHIRE MOORLANDS CHALLENGE WALK
THE LITTLE JOHN CHALLENGE WALK
YORKSHIRE DALES CHALLENGE WALK

NORTH YORKSHIRE MOORS CHALLENGE WALK
LAKELAND CHALLENGE WALK
THE RUTLAND WATER CHALLENGE WALK
MALVERN HILLS CHALLENGE WALK
THE SALTER'S WAY
THE SNOWDON CHALLENGE
CHARNWOOD FOREST CHALLENGE WALK
THREE COUNTIES CHALLENGE WALK (Peak District).
CAL-DER-WENT WALK by Geoffrey Carr,
THE QUANTOCK WAY
BELVOIR WITCHES CHALLENGE WALK
THE CARNEDDAU CHALLENGE WALK
THE SWEET PEA CHALLENGE WALK
THE LINCOLNSHIRE WOLDS - BLACK DEATH - CHALLENGE WALK

INSTRUCTION & RECORD -
HIKE TO BE FIT.....STROLLING WITH JOHN
THE JOHN MERRILL WALK RECORD BOOK
HIKE THE WORLD

MULTIPLE DAY WALKS -
THE RIVERS'S WAY
PEAK DISTRICT: HIGH LEVEL ROUTE
PEAK DISTRICT MARATHONS
THE LIMEY WAY
THE PEAKLAND WAY
COMPO'S WAY by Alan Hiley
THE BRIGHTON WAY by Norman Willis

THE PILGRIM WALKS SERIES -
THE WALSINGHAM WAY - Ely to Walsingham - 72 miles
THE WALSINGHAM WAY - Kings Lynn to Walsingham - 35 miles
TURN LEFT AT GRANJA DE LA MORERUELA - 700 miles
NORTH TO SANTIAGO DE COMPOSTELA, VIA FATIMA - 650 miles
St. OLAV'S WAY - Oslo to Trondheim - 400 miles

COAST WALKS & NATIONAL TRAILS -
ISLE OF WIGHT COAST PATH
PEMBROKESHIRE COAST PATH
THE CLEVELAND WAY
WALKING ANGELSEY'S COASTLINE.
WALKING THE COASTLINE OF THE CHANNEL ISLANDS

DERBYSHIRE & PEAK DISTRICT HISTORICAL GUIDES -
A to Z GUIDE OF THE PEAK DISTRICT
DERBYSHIRE INNS - an A to Z guide
HALLS AND CASTLES OF THE PEAK DISTRICT & DERBYSHIRE
TOURING THE PEAK DISTRICT & DERBYSHIRE BY CAR
DERBYSHIRE FOLKLORE
PUNISHMENT IN DERBYSHIRE
CUSTOMS OF THE PEAK DISTRICT & DERBYSHIRE
WINSTER - a souvenir guide
ARKWRIGHT OF CROMFORD
LEGENDS OF DERBYSHIRE
DERBYSHIRE FACTS & RECORDS
TALES FROM THE MINES by Geoffrey Carr
PEAK DISTRICT PLACE NAMES by Martin Spray
DERBYSHIRE THROUGH THE AGES - Vol 1 -DERBYSHIRE IN PREHISTORIC TIMES
SIR JOSEPH PAXTON
FLORENCE NIGHTINGALE
JOHN SMEDLEY
BONNIE PRINCE CHARLIE & 20 mile walk.
THE STORY OF THE EARLS AND DUKES OF DEVONSHIRE

JOHN MERRILL'S MAJOR WALKS -
TURN RIGHT AT LAND'S END
WITH MUSTARD ON MY BACK
TURN RIGHT AT DEATH VALLEY
EMERALD COAST WALK
JOHN MERRILL'S 1999 WALKER'S DIARY
A WALK IN OHIO - 1,310 miles around the Buckeye Trail.

SKETCH BOOKS -
SKETCHES OF THE PEAK DISTRICT

COLOUR BOOK:-
THE PEAK DISTRICT.......something to remember her by.

OVERSEAS GUIDES -
HIKING IN NEW MEXICO - Vol I - The Sandia and Manzano Mountains.
Vol 2 - Hiking "Billy the Kid" Country. Vol 4 - N.W. area - " Hiking Indian Country."
"WALKING IN DRACULA COUNTRY" - Romania.
WALKING THE TRAILS OF THE HONG KONG ISLANDS.

VISITOR GUIDES - MATLOCK . BAKEWELL. ASHBOURNE.

110

The first crash on Kinder, taken shortly after - Heyford, September 1937.
Photo by Harry Crooks.

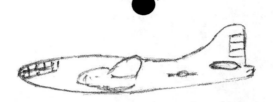

HERE LIES THE WRECKAGE OF B29 SUPERFORTRESS
"OVEREXPOSED" OF THE 16TH PHOTOGRAPHIC RECONNAISSANCE
SQUADRON USAF WHICH TRAGICALLY CRASHED WHILST DESCENDING
THROUGH CLOUD ON 3RD NOVEMBER 1948 KILLING ALL 13
CREW MEMBERS. THE AIRCRAFT WAS ON A ROUTINE FLIGHT
FROM RAF SCAMPTON OF AMERICAN AFB BURTON WOOD.
IT IS DOUBTFUL THE CREW EVER SAW THE GROUND.
MEMORIAL LAID BY 367 AIR NAVIGATION COURSE
OF RAF FINNINGLEY ON 12TH NOVEMBER 1988.

B29 Superfortress plaque, Higher Shelf Stones, Bleaklow.

AIRCRAFT MUSEUMS AND VISITOR'S CENTRE

Newark (Notts & Lincs) Air Museum,
Winthorpe Airfield,
Newark,
Notts.
NG24 2NY

Tel. 01636 - 707170
Has a large range of planes including a Vulcan, Avro Anson, Tiger Moth, and Gloster Meteor. Plus wreckage and engines from a Junkers, Wellington, Lancaster and Halifax.

Battle of Britain Memorial Flight Centre Visitor Centre,
RAF Coningsby,
Lincolnshire
LN4 4SY

Tel. 01526 - 344041
Has a Lancaster, Spitfires, Hurricanes and a Dakota; all of which are maintained and still fly.

Metheringham Airfield Visitor Centre,
Westmoor Farm,
Martin Moor,
Metheringham,
Lincolnshire.
LN4 3BQ

Tel. 01526 - 378270
Museum, Visitor's Centre, Memorial Gardens and flybys.

The Lincolnshire Aviation Heritage Centre,
East Kirkby,
Nr. Spilsby,
Lincolnshire.

Tel - 10790 - 763207
Situated on a 1940's Bomber airfield. Avro Lancaster Bomber and the Barnes Wallis Bouncing Bomb. Visitor Centre.

Avro Anson - Newark Air Museum. August 2004

Gloster Meteor - Newark Air Museum. August 2004

Junkers dispaly and engine - Newark Air Museum. August 2004

Lancaster Bomber Rear Gun turret - Newark Air Museum. August 2004